duction

VERY SHORT INTRODUCTIONS are for anyone wanting a stimulating and accessible way into a new subject. They are written by experts, and have been translated into more than 45 different languages.

The series began in 1995, and now covers a wide variety of topics in every discipline. The VSI library now contains over 500 volumes—a Very Short Introduction to everything from Psychology and Philosophy of Science to American History and Relativity—and continues to grow in every subject area.

Titles in the series include the following:

AFRICAN HISTORY John Parker and
  Richard Rathbone
AMERICAN HISTORY Paul S. Boyer
AMERICAN LEGAL HISTORY
  G. Edward White
AMERICAN POLITICAL PARTIES
  AND ELECTIONS L. Sandy Maisel
AMERICAN POLITICS
  Richard M. Valelly
AMERICAN SLAVERY
  Heather Andrea Williams
ANARCHISM Colin Ward
ANCIENT EGYPT Ian Shaw
ANCIENT GREECE Paul Cartledge
ANCIENT PHILOSOPHY Julia Annas
ANCIENT WARFARE Harry Sidebottom
ANGLICANISM Mark Chapman
THE ANGLO-SAXON AGE John Blair
ANIMAL RIGHTS David DeGrazia
ARCHAEOLOGY Paul Bahn
ARISTOTLE Jonathan Barnes
ART HISTORY Dana Arnold
ART THEORY Cynthia Freeland
ATHEISM Julian Baggini
THE ATMOSPHERE Paul I. Palmer
AUGUSTINE Henry Chadwick
BACTERIA Sebastian G. B. Amyes
BEAUTY Roger Scruton
THE BIBLE John Riches
BLACK HOLES Katherine Blundell
BLOOD Chris Cooper
THE BRAIN Michael O'Shea
THE BRICS Andrew F. Cooper
BRITISH POLITICS Anthony Wright

BUDDHA Michael Carrithers
BUDDHISM Damien Keown
BUDDHIST ETHICS Damien Keown
CAPITALISM James Fulcher
CATHOLICISM Gerald O'Collins
THE CELTS Barry Cunliffe
CHOICE THEORY Michael Allingham
CHRISTIANITY Linda Woodhead
CIRCADIAN RHYTHMS Russell Foster
  and Leon Kreitzman
CITIZENSHIP Richard Bellamy
CLASSICAL MYTHOLOGY
  Helen Morales
CLASSICS Mary Beard and
  John Henderson
CLIMATE CHANGE Mark Maslin
THE COLD WAR Robert McMahon
COMMUNISM Leslie Holmes
CONSCIOUSNESS Susan Blackmore
CONTEMPORARY ART
  Julian Stallabrass
COSMOLOGY Peter Coles
THE CRUSADES Christopher Tyerman
DADA AND SURREALISM
  David Hopkins
DARWIN Jonathan Howard
THE DEAD SEA SCROLLS
  Timothy Lim
DECOLONIZATION Dane Kennedy
DEMOCRACY Bernard Crick
DESIGN John Heskett
DREAMING J. Allan Hobson
DRUGS Les Iversen
THE EARTH Martin Redfern

Leslie Holmes

COMMUNISM

A Very Short Introduction

OXFORD
UNIVERSITY PRESS

OXFORD

UNIVERSITY PRESS

Great Clarendon Street, Oxford OX2 6DP

Oxford University Press is a department of the University of Oxford.
It furthers the University's objective of excellence in research, scholarship,
and education by publishing worldwide in

Oxford New York

Auckland Cape Town Dar es Salaam Hong Kong Karachi
Kuala Lumpur Madrid Melbourne Mexico City Nairobi
New Delhi Shanghai Taipei Toronto

With offices in

Argentina Austria Brazil Chile Czech Republic France Greece
Guatemala Hungary Italy Japan Poland Portugal Singapore
South Korea Switzerland Thailand Turkey Ukraine Vietnam

Oxford is a registered trade mark of Oxford University Press
in the UK and in certain other countries

Published in the United States
by Oxford University Press Inc., New York

© Leslie Holmes 2009

The moral rights of the author have been asserted
Database right Oxford University Press (maker)

First published 2009

British Library Cataloguing in Publication Data

Data available

Library of Congress Cataloging in Publication Data

Data available

Typeset by SPI Publisher Services, Pondicherry, India
Printed in Great Britain by
Ashford Colour Press Ltd., Gosport, Hampshire.

ISBN 978-0-19-955154-5

14

For Lü Qiongyan, Zhou Shimin,
Zhou Yan, and Zhou Tao.

Contents

Preface

Something strange happened in July 2008. The President of the United States, a country that had for decades seen Communism as its principal enemy, looked happy and relaxed as he sat with Chinese Communist leaders at the opening of the Olympic Games in Beijing. In some ways, it was symptomatic of changes both in attitudes in the West towards Communism, and in the nature of Communist power itself. After all, Chinese Communism had become the *Wunderkind* (wonder child) – the development model everyone was talking about – of the late 20th and early 21st centuries, but at the expense of some of what many believed were key aspects of Communism. In fact, Communist China was not only showing the rest of the world how a country could have impressively high economic growth rates year after year, but was actually using some of the results of this growth to invest in capitalist countries, including the USA. This has been one of the great contradictions of recent years.

This is a book about contrasts and contradictions. It is a book about a dream – communism – that for too many became a nightmare; whether we look at Stalin's Terror, Mao's Great Leap Forward and Cultural Revolution, or Pol Pot's genocidal regime in Cambodia, we see millions suffering physical and psychological horrors in the name of what was supposed to be the construction of the fairest and most desirable type of society ever known to humanity. It is a book about a 19th-century idea that many attempted to realize in the 20th century; but in their endeavours to turn it into reality, the original idea became so seriously distorted that, to a large extent, it was discredited. It is a book about a system that, at its zenith, ruled more than a third of the world's population across four continents, and threatened to destroy the West. Yet most of that system eventually, and very suddenly, mutated into spectacular failure. The overwhelming majority of states that were Communist as recently as the late 1980s have now moved on. While, formally, five Communist states remain, the two successful ones (China and Vietnam) are so largely because they have jettisoned many of the original basic tenets of communism and are in some important areas – notably the economy – already post-communist, which helps to explain the conundrum identified in the opening paragraph. A third state – Laos – is still a largely agrarian country, and thus cannot be deemed a success in terms of communism's own objectives. Moreover, like its larger Asian 'Communist' neighbours, Laos has been introducing radical reforms that are moving it away from any traditional conception of a Communist state. The two remaining states (Cuba and North Korea) have by some criteria adhered more closely to the original tenets. But they are weak – and in both cases may be on their way to adopting more and more capitalist principles anyway.

It is not only in the former and still existing Communist states where fundamental contradictions and contrasts can be observed, however. Having smugly claimed victory over Communism at the beginning of the 1990s, the West had within less than two decades entered a crisis period itself, taking everyone else with it. The most radical market-oriented version of capitalism – neo-liberalism – experienced a serious loss of credibility, as millions across the globe suffered economic hardship and uncertainty as a result of the fallout of the near collapse of the Western financial system, and lost faith in it. If the symbol of Communism's failure was the fall of the Berlin Wall, that of the failure of neo-liberalism was the near collapse of Wall Street – Wall-to-Wall contradictions, crisis and failure!

Moreover, by late 2008, the amazon.com ranking of book sales revealed that one of the most difficult books of communist theory to read, Marx's *Capital* (especially Vol. 1), had become a best-seller. And a January 2009 article in Melbourne's leading newspaper *The Age*, referring to the re-registration of the Australian Communists (who had deregistered in July 1990), opened with the sentence 'Dust off your berets and polish your lapel pins – the Communists are officially back'. While the significance of the alleged 're-birth' of Communism should definitely not be exaggerated, there is renewed interest in both its theory and practice. This is the *raison d'être* of the present slim volume.

Some points of clarification are necessary. First, the status of some states as Communist is disputed. Notably, many would disagree with the inclusion here of various African states. The approach here is a broad – more inclusive – one, and in this I have followed the practice of analysts such as David and Marina Ottaway or Bogdan Szajkowski. This said, the fact that many other specialists, such as Archie Brown, would reject this broader interpretation is implicitly noted in the fact that there is very little in this book on these disputed cases. Second, in order to distinguish the theory of communism from the practice of states claiming to be building communism, the latter will be identified in this book by the use of an upper-case 'C' whenever the term 'Communist' is used.

I wish to thank the four anonymous readers of the original book proposal and manuscript for their numerous insightful and sensible suggestions (and corrections!), and the team at Oxford University Press, especially Andrea Keegan and Emma Marchant, for their support throughout this project; at the end of the day, of course, I am solely responsible for any remaining errors and omissions, and for all interpretations. Finally, special thanks to my wife Becky for her support, encouragement, and unfailing good humour during the writing of this book; I owe her more than she realizes.

Leslie Holmes

List of illustrations

Communism

List of tables

Chapter 1
The theory of communism

One of the contradictions in communism most frequently
highlighted is that between the theory and the practice. While this
is to some extent justified, it also needs to be borne in mind that,
as with most concepts, there is no single theory of communism.
Rather, there are numerous theories and variations on a theme –
and some versions of the theory are more compatible with the
practice than others. This theoretical diversity exists not only
because so many individuals have contributed their ideas to the
concept of communism, but also because of gaps, ambiguities, and
even contradictions within the works of some of the best-known
theorists. Nevertheless, there is sufficient agreement among
most analysts of communist theory to permit the drawing of a
reasonably coherent picture. Since this book is primarily
concerned with the practice of Communism, the emphasis here is
on those aspects of theory that provide a better understanding of
how Communists in power perceived the world, why they acted as
they did, and how they attempted to justify their actions.

While there were many theorists of various kinds of communism
both before him (e.g. Henri de Saint-Simon, 1760–1825; Charles
Fourier, 1772–1837) and as contemporaries (e.g. Pierre-Joseph
Proudhon, 1809–65), the person almost always seen nowadays as the
father of communism is Karl Marx (1818–83). In fact, however,

Marx's main contributions were to provide a broad theoretical framework for interpreting the world – in particular, the march of history – and a deep analysis of the nature of capitalism. In many ways, more influential on Communism in practice were the Russian revolutionary leader Vladimir Lenin (1870–1924); his successor, Josef Stalin (1878–1953); and Chinese revolutionary leader Mao Zedong (1893–1976). The contribution of each to communist theory needs to be considered. First, however, it is important to note that – in the cases of Marx, Lenin, and Mao at least – the interest in communism was to no small extent the result of a profound alienation from the existing system and a desire for a better world.

Marxism

Much of what is usually called classical Marxism was in fact based on the ideas of Marx himself and his colleague Friedrich Engels (1820–95). But Marx was the dominant partner in this intellectual relationship, so that we shall follow the usual custom of describing even their co-authored works as Marxist, and the focus here will be on Marx himself.

As with any thinker, it is important to locate Marx in time and place. He was born in what is now Germany – though he spent most of his adult life in England – at a time when the Industrial Revolution and the development of capitalism were already underway in Western Europe. It was also a time when the ramifications of the French Revolution (from 1789) were still being felt throughout Europe, and there were several other revolutionary phases during his lifetime, notably in 1830, 1848–9, and 1871. Marx was fascinated by these various revolutionary situations, and believed he could discern patterns in historical development. These patterns were formed by reactions to events and developments; once the reaction had occurred, there were in turn reactions to this. Marx's approach to history has thus been called a dialectical one, meaning that he saw history progressing through conflict, or the interplay between actions and reactions – while his conviction that there are identifiable laws to the march of history has led many to label him an historicist, and his approach to history historical materialism. This last term requires explanation.

In their attempts to explain the nature of reality, philosophers are often classified as either idealists or materialists. The core of the first of these terms is the word 'idea'. In this approach, the world around us comprises manifestations of concepts or ideas; it is the ideas that constitute reality, not their worldly manifestations. The best-known idealist is the German philosopher G. W. F. Hegel (1770–1831). While Marx was heavily influenced and impressed by Hegel, he adopted a fundamentally different approach to reality. For Marx, the physical – or material (hence materialism) – world around us is reality, and our ideas and perceptions are determined by our relationship to that reality. How we see that world – how we interpret material reality – varies according to who we are, and when and where we live. For instance, one's interpretation or conception of what a city is would be very different if one lived in New York in the 21st century – when we might think of skyscrapers, freeways, subways, congestion, pollution, jazz clubs, and so on – from what it would have been to someone living in Florence in the 15th century or Athens in ancient Greece. The material nature of these three cities in three different eras varies enormously, which in turn affects perceptions of what a city is. But Marx believed that there was more than just temporal and geographic dimensions for explaining differing perceptions. In addition, he argued, a person's position in society affects the way that person perceives the world. For example, the owner of a factory would see the factory in a different light from how a worker in that factory would see it. For the former, it might represent personal achievement, prestige, and high income; for the latter, it might represent alienation, and hard work for a meagre income.

Marx's materialist view of the world is closely related to his historicism; his combination of the two explains why his approach is so often described as historical materialism. For Marx, the driving force of history is class relationships. He defines class in terms of a person's relationship to the means of production; crudely, this means that most people's class position is determined primarily by whether or not they own property, particularly property that can generate wealth. Thus, in the feudal system that preceded the Industrial Revolution and the emergence of capitalism, the most fundamental class division was between those who owned land, and those who had to work for those who owned the land. With the advent of the spinning jenny, the steam engine, and other inventions of the early Industrial Revolution, the most important class division became that between those who owned factories, and those who worked for the factory owners. Marx called the former 'capitalists' or 'the bourgeoisie', and the latter the 'proletariat', which literally means 'without property'. While his class analysis is more complex and sophisticated than the simplified outline provided here, it is these most basic divisions within any given era – centred on private property – that, for Marx, lead to fundamental or revolutionary change. This argument is summarized in the opening chapter of what is the most famous and most widely read book on communism, the short *Communist Manifesto* (1848) – 'The history of all hitherto existing society is the history of class struggles.' According to this theory, the tensions between classes build up over time, and eventually result in revolutionary change. However, until the emergence of capitalism, it was not tensions between what he saw as the main exploiting and the main exploited classes that led to revolutionary change; often, scientific, technical, and economic changes led to the emergence of a new elite that sought to wrest power from the existing ruling class. For Marx, the French Revolution could largely be understood in these terms.

However, Marx believed that the era in which he was living was different from all previous ones, in two ways. First, the class structure of capitalism was becoming simpler than that in earlier epochs, with society even more clearly dominated by just two main classes. Second, the class struggle under capitalism would be primarily between the bourgeoisie and an increasingly alienated

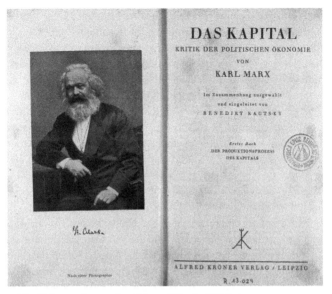

1. Karl Marx and an early edition of *Capital* (Vol. 1)

proletariat, not between the existing ruling class (the bourgeoisie) and some new potential elite class. He believed for most of his life that the tensions between these two main classes would eventually build up to such a point that a socialist revolution would occur. Unlike all previous class revolutions, therefore, this one would be followed by a political system dominated by the *majority* of the population, not a minority or small elite as in the past.

But Marx was vague about what would follow a socialist revolution. He maintained that, *in the long term*, a new type of society – communism – would emerge, in which there would be no ruling class and no alienation. Indeed, in this ultimate society, there would be no politics as such and no need for a state, which would 'wither away'; the 'government of persons' would be replaced by the 'administration of things'. But immediately following the socialist revolution, before this ultimate stage was reached, there would be a temporary or transitional state, the dictatorship of the proletariat. What Marx meant by this is not entirely clear; he only used the actual phrase twice in his writings, and never provided much detail on it. But he was impressed by the short-lived experiment in France known as the Paris Commune (1871), and saw many features of that experiment, including the way in which ordinary workers exercised power – became the new ruling class – as indicative of what a dictatorship of the proletariat might look like.

An important point to emphasize about Marx is that he was above all a theorist and polemicist; while he was politically active at several points in his life, he was not a national leader. This helps to explain why much of his writing and analysis is abstract, and short on practical details. As already noted, his descriptions of the state following a socialist revolution are hazy. However, three important points need to be made before moving on to Lenin. First, Marx was reasonably clear that only advanced industrial societies could have socialist revolutions; predominantly rural, agricultural societies would not be ready for such changes, and history had to follow its own logic. Second, Marx was consistently an internationalist; he did not believe that one country alone could have a successful socialist revolution. Finally and importantly, there is a common misperception that Marx's references to communism were only to the final end-goal. In fact, Marx made it clear in *The German Ideology* (completed in 1846) that communism meant for him the political movement that undermines and overthrows the existing political system as much as the final goal:

> Communism is for us not a *state of affairs* that is to be established, an *ideal* to which reality [will] have to adjust itself. We call communism the *real* movement that abolishes the present state of things. [emphasis in original]

Leninism

Lenin was born in the late 19th century into a Russian family that lived in a small city on the River Volga. Both of his parents were teachers, and had highly developed senses of civic responsibility. When Lenin was just a teenager, his older (but still teenage) brother was arrested and subsequently executed for allegedly plotting to assassinate Tsar Alexander III; a number of commentators have argued that this traumatic experience hardened the young Lenin and helps to explain his passionate hatred of the Russian Tsarist autocracy. This combination of a sense of social responsibility and hatred of the system in which he lived helps to explain Lenin's approach to politics, history, and the Russian Empire.

Soon after the death of his brother, Lenin began to study revolutionary ideas, in particular those of Russian radicals such as Nikolai Chernyshevsky and of Marx. By the late 19th century, he had fallen foul of the Russian authorities, and was sent into exile. But his influence on Russian radicals was profound, and by the end of 1917, following the third Russian Revolution of the 20th century (the October Revolution; there were also revolutions in 1905 and February 1917), he and his party – the Bolsheviks – had taken power. Russia was now to be ruled by Communists for more than seven decades.

Unlike Marx, Lenin was deeply involved in national politics, and while he did occasionally produce more abstract analyses of his longer-term vision of socialism and communism, notably in *The State and Revolution* (1917), most of his contributions to communist theory arose out of his own experiences of and reactions to the world around him, as well as from his polemics with other Marxists. His most important theoretical contributions were on the role of the revolutionary party; his analysis of imperialism; and the distinctions he drew between socialism and communism.

Marx had said little about political parties, in part because they had not been as salient a feature in his day as they became in the 20th century. But Lenin believed that political consciousness of its exploited situation would be slow to develop in the Russian working class, and hence developed his theory of the vanguard party. In *What is to be Done?* (1902), Lenin argued that some people are much more politically aware than others, and should assume responsibility for leading society to socialism. This was an elitist approach to a political party, and has been compared to Plato's arguments in favour of rule by 'philosopher-kings'. Moreover, the party was to be highly secretive. While some have defended Lenin's position on the grounds that the type of clandestine and closed party he advocated was necessary in the repressive conditions of the Tsarist autocracy of the early 20th century, the fact is that the Bolshevik party – which eventually became the Communist Party of the Soviet Union – did not change many of its key features even *after* it had seized power. Indeed, Lenin called for much stricter discipline

2. Vasili Yefanov's portrait of Vladimir Lenin, leader of the October 1917 Russian Revolution

within the party in 1921, long after the monarchy had been overthrown. His elitist and secretive conception of a communist party was one of his most significant legacies.

Lenin's theory of imperialism is particularly relevant here because it ultimately led to the justification of a significant change to Marx's approach – one that was subsequently used by revolutionaries in many parts of the world to justify their seizure of power in situations Marx himself would have considered quite inappropriate. In a long analysis of the reasons for the outbreak of World War I published in 1917, Lenin maintained that imperialism was 'the highest stage of capitalism'. The world's major empires had essentially divided up the world between them and, according to Lenin, the only way individual imperial powers could now continue to expand in their search for resources, new markets, and cheap labour was to seize colonies from other imperial powers. Lenin saw this constant drive for expansion and profit as the basis of the conflict between major European powers that constituted the Great War. The relevance of this to the development of Communism is that Lenin used his theory to justify the Bolshevik takeover of power in Russia, despite his awareness that, according to classical Marxist analysis, Russia was not yet ready for a socialist revolution. He argued that Russia, which had begun its industrialization in earnest in the late 19th century but was still overwhelmingly an agrarian country, constituted the weakest link in a chain of capitalist countries; if the chain were to be broken at its weakest point, the whole edifice of international capitalism would collapse. Russia would then be absorbed into the new international socialist orbit by the countries that *were* sufficiently developed to move on from capitalism, such as Britain, France, and Germany. By the early 1920s, it was clear that capitalism had not collapsed; but the Bolsheviks were unwilling to surrender the power they had seized in October 1917, and Lenin had made a significant change to classical Marxist theory.

A final point about Lenin's contribution to communist theory is that he drew a sharper distinction than Marx did between socialism and communism. Marx often used the terms interchangeably, although he did sometimes describe the former as the early phase of the latter. But Lenin was more explicit that the distribution of wealth under socialism was to be on a different basis from that under communism; whereas the guiding principle under the latter was to be 'from each according to their ability, to each according to their need', under the former it was to be 'from each according to their ability, to each according to their labour'. This distinction has been used to justify sometimes significant differences in income in Communist states. Lenin also placed more emphasis than Marx did on the need for a strong state immediately following a socialist revolution, which subsequently played into the hands of Communists in power.

Stalinism

Lenin died in January 1924, and a salient feature of Communist systems – their inability or unwillingness to introduce formal leadership succession arrangements – immediately became obvious. By the late 1920s, the Georgian Stalin had won the leadership succession struggle against rivals such as Leon Trotsky; Stalin's image until then as a moderate compromiser was in marked contrast to that of Trotsky, who was seen as a brilliant but often hotheaded and ruthless intellectual. Stalin's conciliatory image was ironic since, once he had consolidated power, he emerged as one of the cruelest dictators in history. Although not possessed of a highly original intellect, Stalin did contribute to communist theory, and sometimes justified his actions (practice) through quasi-theoretical means.

Stalin's most important contribution to communist theory was in his advocacy and adoption of the notion of 'Socialism in One Country' in 1925–6. This was not a particularly insightful concept, since it

3. Josef Stalin

represented little more than a theoretical justification of actual developments in and beyond what had since 1922 been called the Union of Soviet Socialist Republics (USSR). Nor was it Stalin who originally devised the concept; while he had made vague references along these lines in late 1924, it was another of his rivals for the top leadership position, Nikolai Bukharin, who really developed the idea, which Stalin then adopted as official policy. The policy basically justified attempts to build socialism not only in one country, but also in a country that Lenin had admitted was not, by itself, ready for socialism. The policy thus contradicted two basic tenets of classical Marxism. On the other hand, it appealed to Soviet citizens much more than Trotsky's notion of permanent revolution; most citizens were tired of wars and revolutions, and wanted stability. Socialism in One Country was also used to justify the introduction of other key features of Stalin's approach, and which became salient aspects of Communist systems. These were industrialization via a centrally planned economy, and collectivization of agriculture. Although it would be stretching a point to argue that two further features of Stalinism – high levels of state terror and a personality cult – were part of communist theory, they did become salient features of Communist practice in many other countries.

Marxism–Leninism

Although the term was not used by Lenin, Communist ideology was often called 'Marxism-Leninism', a term apparently devised by Stalin. Some Communist states made additions to this term to give their ideology a national or local flavour. Thus Chinese ideology was long called 'Marxism-Leninism and Mao Zedong Thought' – though this has now been updated to incorporate the contribution of Mao's successors, and has since late 2002 been known by the unwieldy title of 'Marxism-Leninism, Mao Zedong Thought, Deng Xiaoping Theory, and the Thought of Three Represents' (the Chinese Communist Party must always represent 'the development trend of China's advanced productive forces, the orientation of China's advanced culture, and the fundamental interests of the overwhelming majority of the Chinese people', according to former Chinese supreme leader Jiang Zemin). Similarly, North Korean ideology has been labelled 'Marxism-Leninism and the Juche Idea'; Juche is a Korean conception of self-reliance, and clearly resonates with Stalin's Socialism in One Country.

Maoism

Like Lenin, Mao was attracted to Marxism because of his profound dissatisfaction with the situation in his country in his earlier years; but he was particularly attracted to Lenin's theory of imperialism and Stalin's notion of Socialism in One Country. China had overthrown the imperial system in the 1911 Chinese Revolution, but had then entered a period of rule by warlords and nationalists that, as Mao saw it, was not helping the country's development.

According to contemporary Chinese ideologists, Mao's major contribution to communist theory was to develop a theoretical justification for the building of and rule by a Communist party in a 'semi-colonial, semi-feudal society comprising mainly peasants and petty bourgeoisie'. Although Stalin distorted classical Marxism in various ways, he did accept that the Marxist model was based on an urban proletariat, not the rural peasantry; indeed, although this quotation is often cited out of context, Marx and Engels had referred in *The Communist Manifesto* to 'the idiocy of rural life'. But Mao took power in an overwhelmingly agricultural country, and needed to justify his claim that this was in line with Marxism. In fact, he was better able to legitimize his actions and ideas in terms of 'Marxism-Leninism' – particularly Stalin's notion of Socialism in One Country – than of classical Marxism.

Eurocommunism

Lenin, Stalin, and Mao all elaborated their theories in the context of what would nowadays be called developing states. But given Marx's own focus on advanced industrial states, it is important not to overlook the fact that Western states such as France and Italy had powerful Communist parties for much of the 20th century. However, conditions in these and other Western countries differed significantly from those in the USSR, China, and other Communist states, so that it is hardly surprising that some Communists in Western Europe developed a quite different approach to communism. While some, notably in France, remained loyal to Moscow from the 1940s until at least the late 1960s, others soon began to question the suitability of the Soviet model for their own countries and conditions. Leading this were the Italians. Already in the 1950s, Italian Communist leader Palmiro Togliatti had argued that it was inappropriate for Communists to revere one country or system, and that each country should develop its own blueprint for achieving communism, depending on its specific circumstances. He therefore advocated 'polycentrism', rather than a world Communist movement focused on one centre (i.e. Moscow). This initially received only limited support among other Western Communist parties. But the Soviet-led Warsaw Pact invasion of Czechoslovakia in August 1968 led to widespread criticism of the USSR among Western Communists generally, not only the Italians. Many left their parties in disgust. Others, however, preferred to remain in their parties, criticize Soviet Communism, and develop their own softer and more democratic version of Communism. One other spur to the emergence of what by the mid-1970s was being called 'Eurocommunism' was the collapse of the right-wing Franco dictatorship in Spain and the re-emergence of the Spanish Communist Party. While many other Communist parties in Western Europe were also more or less attracted to the new, more tolerant and less dogmatic version of communism, it was really the French, Italian, and Spanish parties – particularly the latter two – that led the way. Although the movement eventually faded, with most Italian Communists even abandoning the term 'communism' altogether and re-naming themselves the Democratic Party of the Left in 1991, it had constituted a serious intellectual and theoretical challenge to Communists in power in Eastern Europe, the USSR, and Asia for much of the 1970s and 1980s.

Conclusions

Communist theory is ambiguous, often incomplete, and sometimes overtly contradictory. This is partly because the various theorists were writing at different times about different conditions and in different personal situations; not being a political leader himself, Marx did not have to justify his actions – unlike Lenin, Stalin, or Mao. It is partly because they were sometimes interpreting the past, sometimes analysing the present, sometimes discussing the near-to-medium-term future, and occasionally speculating on the long-term goal of a communist society. In part it is also because, like most theorists, they were not completely consistent throughout their lives. And in part, it is because they were sometimes writing from a more normative perspective (i.e. what should be), at other times from a more descriptive one (i.e. what is).

But in addition, there are also fundamental differences of approach among communist theorists, which are best explained in terms of the voluntarism versus determinism debate. Marx himself mostly tended towards a determinist interpretation of history, meaning that he believed history had to work its way through its various stages – the actions and reactions of the dialectic. While he believed that Communists could and should help to keep the pace of historical change moving – 'the philosophers have only *interpreted* the world . . . the point is to *change* it', he wrote in *Theses on Feuerbach* (completed 1845) – Marx was wary of what might happen if they attempted artificially to accelerate it too much. Indeed, Marx became more of a determinist in his later years. In his never completed major analysis of the political economy of capitalism, *Capital* (Vol. 1 published 1867; the incomplete Vols. 2 and 3 were edited by Engels and published posthumously in 1885 and 1894 respectively), Marx describes a more abstract, impersonal, and globalized capitalism, in which the structural contradictions inherent within the system itself, rather than a conscious struggle between capitalists and workers, leads to crisis and the collapse of capitalism.

Conversely, leaders such as Lenin and Mao were clearly voluntarists, in that they believed that the application of human will could and would accelerate or even bypass historical processes. Whether they were voluntarists because of their assertive personalities, or because of a perceived need to use a revolutionary theory to justify their actions to overthrow repressive regimes and modernize their societies, or – most likely – because of a blend of these, the fact remains that they adapted Marxism to suit their objectives. In the process, they distorted the original ideas – even more so Marx's later writing than his earlier theorizing. For this, they were sometimes criticized by other, more determinist Marxists; the German–Austrian Karl Kautsky (1854–1938) was often highly critical of Lenin's voluntarism, for instance. This said, and as has been shown, Marx's own writings on socialist revolution and what would follow this were often vague or incomplete, so that they lent themselves to very diverse interpretations. But there are tensions and contradictions even within Lenin's work, and his views on what would succeed a socialist revolution as expressed in *The State and Revolution* were sometimes at odds with what he wrote and did following what he claimed was a socialist revolution in Russia. Given all this, the best way to understand what Communism is or was is to study it in practice.

Chapter 2
A brief history of communism in power

By the 1970s, more than a third of the world's population lived in a Communist system. But the process by which this had occurred took several decades, and there were numerous challenges to it along the way.

From 1917 to World War II

The second (October) Russian Revolution of 1917 is generally taken as the starting point of Communism in power. The first 1917 Russian Revolution had occurred in February, and had brought down the centuries'-old Tsarist autocracy. For several months following that, Russia had been ruled by a provisional government. But this government had not performed well, and the one major political party that had not participated in it was able to criticize it and eventually bring it down. That party was the Bolshevik (meaning 'majoritarian') party, led by Vladimir Lenin; it was to become the first ruling Communist party in the world.

The Bolsheviks were Marxists, but of a particular sort. Early in the 20th century, they had been joined with another group in a single political party. But this party split in the early 1900s, largely because the Bolsheviks were voluntarists, whereas the other group – the Mensheviks ('minoritarians') – believed that significant problems could arise if the pace of historical change were to be artificially accelerated. But the Russian populace was tired of World War I and the various privations this involved, and Lenin's simple but powerful slogan – 'Peace, Land, Bread' – appealed to large numbers of Russians in both the cities and the villages.

But many Russians opposed the new regime under Lenin, and mobilized to counter it. There was thus a civil war in Russia between 1917 and 1921. The Bolsheviks eventually won this. But they soon realized that their problems were far from over, as some of their own erstwhile supporters began to question and challenge them. This culminated in the Kronstadt Rebellion of 1921, in which sailors and workers on the outskirts of what is now St Petersburg demanded that the Bolsheviks start sharing political power and conversing more with those they were supposed to represent. But the Bolshevik leadership was in no mood to make concessions to the rebels, and sent a contingent of some 60,000 soldiers to suppress the Kronstadt revolt. Although the Bolsheviks' counter-attack was successful – if very bloody – the party's leaders acknowledged that they were in danger of losing the popular support they had so recently enjoyed. Their honeymoon was over, and a new approach was needed.

The end of the Kronstadt Rebellion coincided with the Tenth Congress of the Party, at which this new approach was decided. The chosen solution appeared to involve diametrically opposed policies. In the political sphere, the Communists clamped down. This could be seen clearly in two ways. First, they now banned other political parties; although it is often assumed that the Soviet regime was a one-party system from the start, the Bolsheviks not only did not initially (i.e. in 1917 and 1918) ban other parties, but were even in a coalition with another party that had widespread support among the peasantry, the Left Social Revolutionaries. But from 1921 onwards, and although this was never formalized as a constitutional requirement, what was in 1922 officially to become the Union of Soviet Socialist Republics (USSR, or Soviet Union) was a one-party state. The second symbol of a political clampdown was that the senior leadership under Lenin now forbade factionalism *within* the party. In future, party members would be breaking party rules if they attempted to form subgroups to challenge or even question the senior leaders' policies and decisions.

But the Bolsheviks adopted a quite different approach to the economy. Instead of tightening up as they had in the political sphere, they now liberalized, adopting the so-called New Economic Policy (NEP). This involved encouraging small-scale capitalist enterprise and private trade; the Bolsheviks hoped that if the economic situation in the country improved as a result of this new policy, then much of the disappointment being felt by their own supporters would evaporate.

It is impossible to know how much longer the NEP would have lasted had Lenin remained alive and the leader of the Communists. But the mastermind of the Russian Revolution suffered his first stroke in 1922, and was increasingly incapacitated thereafter; he died in January 1924. Since the Bolsheviks had not adopted any succession mechanism, the new leader emerged as a result of a prolonged power struggle. The main competitors in this were Nikolai Bukharin, Leon Trotsky, and Josef Stalin, though Bukharin soon dropped out of the race. Perhaps ironically, many of the senior Bolsheviks considered Trotsky too clever – and therefore potentially dangerous – to be the supreme leader. In contrast, Stalin had appeared to be more conciliatory; one of his leading biographers, Isaac Deutscher, describes Stalin's image at this time as 'the man of the golden mean'. Moreover, Stalin's policy of Socialism in One Country held far greater appeal to most Soviet citizens and Communists than Trotsky's concept of permanent revolution. People had had enough of war (World War I; Civil War) and revolutionary change, so that it is not surprising that the notion of continuous upheaval was unattractive. Conversely, Stalin's approach appealed to many. By arguing that the Soviet Union did not need to risk foreign invasion by trying to export revolution, Stalin was able to calm popular fears of further turmoil. Moreover, by claiming that the USSR would become the first country in the world to achieve a system that was more advanced than any Western capitalist one, he was able to play on both the dreams and the nationalism of many of his subjects. There can be little doubt that, as of the mid-1920s, many Soviet citizens were enthusiastic about the future of their country. Under certain circumstances, Communism can be an inspirational ideology.

But the dreams associated with Socialism in One Country had by the mid-1930s largely become nightmares. From the late 1920s, Stalin began to introduce policies designed to achieve his particular version of socialism. Since it was to be built in one country, and since the rest of the world was basically hostile to that country's system, he would have to construct his model using only domestic building blocks. It was in this context that the USSR introduced five-year plans, industrialization, collectivization – and, eventually, the terror machine.

The Communists' introduction of the NEP in 1921 was designed to kick-start the economy after the problems of World War I and the Russian Civil War. The leadership had always intended it to be a temporary measure, though the timeframe was unclear at the time of its introduction. Nikolai Bukharin, for example, had argued that socialism could emerge in the USSR only at the pace of a 'peasant nag'; unless the peasantry – still by far the largest group in the population – could be persuaded of the need for and pace of change, there could be a backlash. Despite this, Lenin had in 1921 established an agency that was in time to act as a central planning agency. This was *Gosplan* (State Planning Office). While this body did little in Lenin's time, its establishment meant that there already existed both a commitment to planning and an agency to direct this by the time Stalin had consolidated power in the late 1920s.

The start of the post-NEP era is disputed, but is commonly taken as 1928, since it was in October of that year that the Soviet Union adopted its first five-year economic plan. Initially, the plan focused on Soviet industrialization; although Russian industrial development and urbanization had developed impressively from the 1880s and 1890s, the country was still a predominantly agrarian and rural one in the late 1920s. Since Marx had argued that socialism could only be built in advanced industrial societies, Stalin could with some justification claim that Socialism in One Country required a major industrialization and urbanization drive. Thus was born the first Communist economic plan.

Given the focus on industrial development, the first version of the plan did not target agriculture. But it soon became clear that any major industrialization drive would need massive investment. Since overseas investors were unwilling to assist a Communist state's economic development, the funds would have to be generated domestically. In capitalist states, large-scale investment is often generated by the private sector, the bourgeoisie. But the numerically small pre-revolutionary Russian bourgeoisie had largely fled the country or been killed between 1917 and 1921, and the NEP, while reasonably successful, had not generated sufficient private wealth to fund the scale of development envisaged by Stalin. Nor did the state itself have investment funds on the scale required for such a massive development programme. The Communists would have to look elsewhere for their funding.

It was in this situation that Stalin soon looked to the peasantry to fund his ambitious programme. After all, this was the largest section of the population, and it was unclear that the funds could be generated from any other source. Stalin sought to justify his new (from 1929) focus on the peasantry in two ways. First, he sought their support for the building of a better society in which everybody, peasants included, would be much better off. Second, the principal means he intended to use in order to generate new wealth – extracting surplus from the peasantry via greater agricultural efficiency and profitability, which were to be achieved through collectivization – would encourage individually oriented peasants to work and think in more collective ways. In short, he hoped to kill two birds with one stone: the generation of new funds for industrial development, and the development of a more collective or socialist consciousness among the peasantry.

Unfortunately, this cosy equation was unrealistic. The second word in the powerful slogan 'Peace, Land, Bread' was directed primarily at the peasantry, since Lenin appreciated that most peasants wanted to run their own farms. Although the peasantry was supposed to have been liberated under the 1861 Serf Emancipation Act, many farmers had in fact found themselves increasingly in debt as the decades passed. For them, much of the attraction of the Bolsheviks had been the promise of their own debt-free farms. Moreover, the NEP had encouraged a form of individual entrepreneurship that appealed to many. Thus Stalin's proposal to develop a more socialist consciousness among the peasantry conflicted with the fact that many farmers had only relatively recently achieved the kind of independence they had sought for centuries and which they were unwilling to give up. While Russian tradition indicated that many were willing to cooperate with each other if they themselves chose to do so, they did not want to be forced into this by the state. Serious tensions were bound to arise. Stalin soon became aware of this reluctance, and from 1930 *coerced* peasants into joining collective farms (i.e. farms in which the equipment, livestock, seeds, and so on were jointly rather than individually owned). Not surprisingly, many peasants resented this coercion and became increasingly anti-Communist.

By 1934, Stalin had claimed victory in converting the countryside. Yet millions had died during 1932–3 as a result of a famine for which Stalin was held largely responsible, and even many of his own colleagues criticized him for going too far, too fast. Opposition and criticism had by now built up at various levels in society, including in the highest levels of the Communist leadership. But rather than retreat or compromise, Stalin now opted to deal with opposition in a manner similar to that which Hitler had been using in Germany – the use of extreme arbitrary coercion against 'enemies', real and imagined. So was unleashed one of the darkest periods in the history of Communist power, the Stalin Terror.

Quite how many people lost their lives as a result of the Stalin Terror is still debated, and the precise figures will probably never be known. Part of the problem is that different analysts include or exclude different forms of death and suffering. For instance, if millions die as a result of a failed policy that results in famine, should those deaths be included in the number of victims of the Stalin Terror? Whatever the actual figure – and estimates range between several hundred thousand and 40 million, with 3–5 million being a sober and realistic figure – they were huge numbers by any criterion. The Stalin Terror peaked in 1936–8, though elements of it continued until Stalin's death in March 1953. Before moving to the post-Stalin era, however, it is time to look beyond the USSR to consider the Communist movement and expansion globally.

The spread of communism in the aftermath of World War II

Until the 1940s there was only one Communist system other than the USSR, Mongolia; this had come under Communist control in 1924. There were various attempts at establishing Communist systems elsewhere in the aftermath of World War I, notably in Germany and Hungary, but these had ultimately come to naught. This situation changed dramatically in the 1940s. By the end of that decade, Communists were in power in most of Eastern Europe and much of East Asia.

Like the USA, the USSR did not enter World War II until 1941; like the USA, it did so as a reaction to invasion. But an important difference between the American and Soviet situations was that, unlike the USA, the USSR had signed a non-aggression treaty with its potential aggressor. Under the 1939 Molotov–Ribbentrop Pact, Nazi Germany had agreed not to invade the Soviet Union; one of Hitler's biggest mistakes was to renege on this agreement and invade the USSR.

Under the Molotov–Ribbentrop Pact, the USSR had in essence been given the green light by the Nazis to incorporate the Baltic states of Estonia, Latvia, and Lithuania. These had been sovereign independent states between World Wars I and II, but were – together with Moldavia (now Moldova) – added to the USSR in 1940. In a real sense, this was the first expansion of Communist power that resulted from World War II. But it was only the start; the Soviet Empire was to expand dramatically after the war.

The USSR defended itself bravely against the Nazis and scored a number of successes. Nevertheless, Stalin realized that the fight against fascism would be a tough one, and that it was in his country's interests to cooperate with other anti-fascist forces. Equally, the Western powers were finding the Nazis a more resilient and capable enemy than they had anticipated. Both the Soviet Union and the West therefore decided to put past differences aside for as long as it took to defeat the common enemy. Fascism was eventually defeated in 1945, and it was time to agree on the future architecture of Europe. The allies – primarily the Americans, the British, and the Soviets, though France was also involved in the later stages – had begun to discuss this in Teheran in 1943, but continued their negotiations in Yalta (February 1945) and then Potsdam (July–August 1945). It was during these talks, for instance, that the future of Germany was decided; it would be administered in four zones (American, British, French, and Soviet). While the future division of Germany into a Western-oriented state (West Germany, or the Federal Republic of Germany) and a Soviet-oriented, Communist one (East Germany, or the German Democratic Republic) was not envisaged at this stage – the final division occurred in 1949 – the seeds of this had already been sown. But there is one other meeting that was crucial to the future spread of Communism, and to which the USA was not a party; this was a private meeting between British Prime Minister Winston Churchill and Stalin that took place in Moscow in October 1944. It was at this meeting that the notorious 'percentages agreement' was reached; this agreement was crucial to the future of Eastern Europe.

It was Churchill, not Stalin, who proposed the percentages agreement. Under this, the UK and the USSR essentially agreed to divide up much of Eastern Europe, with the respective countries having differing amounts of 'predominance' in named countries. For instance, Churchill proposed that the Soviet Union would be predominant in Romania and Bulgaria, the UK would be predominant in Greece, and there would be equal power-sharing in Yugoslavia and Hungary. Stalin immediately agreed to this proposal. While not applicable to *all* of Eastern Europe, the agreement did essentially hand Bulgaria and Romania to the Soviets – who, it must be acknowledged, kept their end of the bargain *vis-à-vis* Greece, which would almost certainly have gone Communist after World War II had it not been for Soviet interference. Equally, the Soviets did not play any significant role in the Communist accession to power in Yugoslavia. If the Soviets can be accused of reneging on any part of this agreement – its questionable nature warrants the more loaded term 'deal' – it was only with regard to Hungary. But even in the Hungarian case, the Soviets had been offered 50% predominance by the British leader.

The precise manner in which the Communists came to power varied in each East European state. For example, the Red (Soviet) Army played a crucial and direct role in the cases of Bulgaria and Romania, whereas Stalin had originally hoped that the local Communists would be able to take power in Czechoslovakia legitimately, through the ballot box; unfortunately, much of the enthusiasm the Czechs and Slovaks had displayed for the Communists in 1945 had dissipated by 1948, and Moscow eventually (in 1948) had to support a form of palace coup to ensure Communist victory there. Yugoslavia and Albania were different again; there, it was local Communists who took power themselves, without any Soviet involvement of note. Indeed, the Yugoslav Communists under Tito were aided more by the West than by Moscow.

The spread of Communism after World War II was not confined to Eastern Europe: Communists were also taking power in East and Southeast Asia. By the end of the 1940s, Communists were in power in Vietnam (1945), North Korea (1948), and mainland China (1949). The North Korean situation was somewhat akin to the East German, in that, following Allied victory over the Japanese at the end of World War II, that part of Korea under Soviet control soon became a Communist state, under Kim Il Sung. In the other two cases, however, the local Communists – led by Ho Chi Minh in Vietnam and Mao Zedong in China – took power largely under their own steam, without any significant Soviet assistance. The war had destabilized many countries in the region, and it was in this confusion that the Communists, who were typically better organized than many of their political rivals, were able to seize the reins of power. In China, for instance, Mao was able to lead his Communists against the rival Nationalist Party (*Guomindang*) under Chiang Kai-shek, who fled with his followers to Taiwan.

Thus by the end of the 1940s, the number of states under Communist control had grown dramatically compared with the inter-war period, from just two to thirteen – the original two plus Albania, Bulgaria, China, Czechoslovakia, (East) Germany, Hungary, (North) Korea, Poland, Romania, Vietnam, and Yugoslavia. Most of these were oriented towards Moscow – the one exception being Yugoslavia, which was expelled from the Soviet camp in 1948 – and had begun to adopt Soviet-type policies. This included the nationalization of industry; the adoption of macroeconomic plans; collectivization of agriculture; state provision of free healthcare and education; subsidized housing and public transport; and – last but not least – the use of terror to eliminate actual or perceived enemies.

Stalin's death and cracks in the communist movement

Stalin died in March 1953. Despite his having overseen the single largest terror campaign in history – though in terms of the *percentage* of the population seriously harmed, Pol Pot's terror in Communist Cambodia 1975–9 was even worse – many Soviet citizens were genuinely grief-stricken at his passing. Various explanations have been suggested for this. For some citizens, Stalin's achievements greatly outweighed his flaws; after all, by the time of his death, the USSR was a modern industrial state at the centre of what was in many ways a new empire. Its model of socialism had been adopted in locally tailored ways in numerous countries in Europe and Asia. Some analysts also claim that Russians – the largest ethnic group in the USSR – revere strong leaders, and refer to traditions going back at least to Tsar Ivan the Terrible (16th century) in support of their claims; for those subscribing to such a view, the respect for and even love of Stalin is simply in line with Russian political culture.

Whatever the reasons for widespread grief in the Soviet Union at Stalin's passing, his death meant uncertainty. Since the USSR still had no formal process for replacing leaders, the period following Stalin's death witnessed a power struggle at the top not unlike that following Lenin's death some three decades earlier. The main competitors this time were Gyorgy Malenkov, Vyacheslav Molotov, Lazar Kaganovich, and the man who was eventually victorious in the power struggle, Nikita Khrushchev. Khrushchev finally secured his position after the defeat of the so-called 'anti-party group' in June 1957, so that it had taken more than four years of struggle for the new leadership to emerge. This period was one of tension and upheaval in many parts of the Communist world.

Although there were small outbreaks of dissatisfaction in both Bulgaria and Czechoslovakia shortly after Stalin's death, the first *major* sign of unrest emerged in East Germany in mid-June (1953). A strike by workers in East Berlin complaining about the conditions in their country soon became nationwide. This was forcibly put down by both East German and Soviet forces, and the message soon spread among citizens around the Communist world that they should not imagine they could 'make hay while the sun shines' in the sense of challenging their Communist masters in times of uncertainty. The confusion at the top of the Soviet system was not sufficient to mean that the Communist empire would tolerate threats from its own citizens.

However, the situation appeared to change dramatically in 1956, which was a watershed year in the history of international Communist power. In that year, there was mass unrest in both Poland and Hungary. Although the Soviets did not invade the former to suppress this, they did invade Hungary, resulting in the deaths of some 20,000 citizens. In order to understand the background to this unrest, it is necessary to consider three factors – Khrushchev's attitudes towards Yugoslavia; Togliatti's concept of 'polycentrism'; and Khrushchev's so-called Secret Speech of February 1956.

As mentioned above, a rift developed between Yugoslavia and the USSR in the late 1940s. At least until Stalin's death, relations between these two Communist states were icy. But Khrushchev believed that it was in no one's interest – at least no Communist leader's interest – for two Communist states to be on such bad terms. While the reasons for the original tensions between Moscow and Belgrade are complex, part of the explanation is that Tito and the Yugoslav Communists had taken power without Soviet assistance, and came to resent Moscow trying to dictate their path to Communism. In the years following 1948, the Yugoslav leadership sought to develop their own version of socialism, which was intended to be less centralized, less bureaucratic, and less authoritarian than the Soviet model. This model was known as the 'self-management' approach. By 1955, as his position within the Soviet system was crystallizing, Khrushchev felt confident enough to make it clear that Moscow could and would tolerate the alternative model of socialism being developed in Yugoslavia. In other words, the Soviet leader appeared to acknowledge that other Communist states could choose their own path towards the common end-goal. That was certainly how some in Eastern Europe interpreted Khrushchev's position.

This inference about a marked change in the Soviet position was endorsed when Khrushchev appeared to accept Togliatti's concept of polycentrism. The basic point of this was that Communists should be unified worldwide, but that each country had the right to pursue its own path. Again, Khrushchev's tolerance of this idea sent a message of hope – whether intentionally or not – to many in Eastern Europe who believed that their leaders were being unnecessarily subservient to Moscow.

But what was almost certainly the principal trigger for the 1956 unrest was the speech made by Khrushchev at the 20th Congress of the Communist Party of the Soviet Union in February of that year. This was neither published in the congress proceedings nor reported in the Soviet media; but word of it soon leaked out. The most significant aspect of the speech was that Khrushchev was highly critical of Stalin – in particular for the Terror of the 1930s and for the fact that the USSR suffered even more than was necessary during World War II because Stalin had not prepared the country sufficiently for an invasion. Khrushchev also criticized Stalin for the way he had treated Yugoslavia. While Khrushchev's criticisms were couched in cautious terms – the Soviet leader referred only to Stalin's 'errors' – the message was clear enough. And as reports of it

4. The Hungarian Uprising of 1956

gradually spread around the world, so the pent-up frustration
and anger of large numbers of citizens in two countries in which
the Soviets were seen to have imposed Communism, Poland and
Hungary, burst into the open.

The brutal Soviet suppression of the Hungarian Uprising soon
stopped the further spread of this unrest. It also revealed that it
was acceptable for the Soviet leader to criticize his predecessor, but
not for ordinary folk to do so, let alone for them to challenge their
own leaderships. While both Poland and Hungary acquired new
Communist leaders as a result of the 1956 uprisings, other changes
were very limited.

The impact of the Secret Speech reached far beyond Eastern Europe.
It was a major stimulus to what, by 1960, had clearly emerged as a
fundamental rift between the two giants of the Communist world,
the USSR and China. The Sino-Soviet rift was yet another sign of
significant cracks in the world Communist movement.

The events of 1956 not only led to tensions *within* the Communist bloc. They also alienated many Communists in countries in which they were not in power, and led to a great deal of self-questioning among them. Thousands of Communists in the West and elsewhere reached the conclusion that the Soviet invasion of Hungary had demonstrated that the original ideas and ideals of Marx, and perhaps Lenin, had been either seriously distorted or proven unrealistic, and so left their parties in disillusionment.

According to one's perspective, however, it could be argued that there were real achievements, as well as what *initially* looked like some encouraging signs in the Communist world from the mid-1950s to the early 1960s. Few would deny that the Soviet launch of the world's first space satellite (*Sputnik*) in October 1957 was a feather in the USSR's cap, for instance. But there were also more ambiguous cases. For instance, Khrushchev had in 1954 announced a radical large-scale plan designed to improve Soviet agricultural output by dramatically increasing the amount of land under cultivation. This was the Virgin Lands campaign, so called because it involved cultivating land in southern Russia and northern Kazakhstan that had not previously been used for agriculture. In China, Mao also introduced a radical and large-scale plan to develop agriculture, the Great Leap Forward (GLF, 1958–60). Whereas the massive communization that preceded it in the mid-1950s was in *some* ways analogous to Stalin's collectivization programme of the late 1920s/early 1930s, the GLF represented a radical departure from the Stalinist approach. Mao initially placed far more faith in local initiative and the peasants' willingness to change than Stalin had, and far less faith in centralized planning. And by 1961, Communism had expanded to within 90 miles of the US coastline, as Cuba's revolutionary leader Fidel Castro decided to re-label his takeover of power a socialist revolution and align his country with Moscow. Castro had not originally been a Communist, and certainly was not one when he led the revolutionary overthrow of the corrupt Batista regime in Cuba in 1959. But his conflicts with both Cuba's own bourgeoisie and the USA led him to look for a powerful supporter; despite initial reluctance, or at least hesitation, Moscow soon agreed to back Castro, who declared himself to be a recent convert to communism.

Unfortunately, these dramatic changes soon proved to be much less impressive than the Communist leaderships in the various countries had hoped for. Inadequate preparation and poor management meant that the Virgin Lands had by the early 1960s become in essence a dustbowl. China's Great Leap Forward alienated substantial portions of the population, and resulted in widespread famine and suffering for millions of Chinese. Most estimates of the number of Chinese who died as a result of the Great Leap Forward are in the range of 15 to 30 million. The Great Leap also led to a temporary decline in Mao's position; the once charismatic leader who had been so popular with so many Chinese peasants was now struggling. And developments relating to Cuba had by 1962 resulted in tensions between Washington and Moscow – the Cuban Missile Crisis – so severe that some believed World War III was about to begin. Fortunately, this did not happen; but avoiding war resulted in a major humiliation for Khrushchev and, by implication, the USSR itself. Overall, the early 1960s were not a good period for Communist power.

This said, there were *some* unambiguously encouraging signs. For example, the man who had become the new leader in Hungary after the 1956 invasion, Janos Kadar, proved to be increasingly liberal, at least by Communist standards. A clear symbol of this came in 1961, when he reversed an old Leninist adage; from now on in Hungary it was no longer a case of 'if you're not with us, you're against us' but rather 'if you're not against us, you're with us'. This might sound like a rather precious or trivial word game to those who have never lived under Communist rule. But many Hungarians saw it as a potentially significant change, as long as it was to be respected in practice.

The USSR reasserts itself

Khrushchev's (and the Soviet Union's) international humiliation over the Cuban Missile Crisis of 1962, when the USSR had been forced by US President John F. Kennedy to abandon its plans to install nuclear warheads in Cuba, was only one among many reasons why other senior Soviet leaders plotted to remove him. He was blamed for the failure of the Virgin Lands campaign, and for substantial price increases for meat and butter in 1962. Moreover, Khrushchev had restructured the management of the economy in a way that was disapproved of by many of his more centralism-oriented colleagues. He upset many of them by going further in the early 1960s than in 1956 in his criticisms of Stalin; whereas he referred at the 20th Congress only to Stalin's 'errors', he was by 1961 publicly talking of his predecessor's 'crimes'. In this context, he permitted the publication in 1962 of a short novel by Alexander Solzhenitsyn, *One Day in the Life of Ivan Denisovich*, which was, albeit in an understated way, a damning criticism of Stalin and his terror machine. All this was too much for Khrushchev's fellow leaders who, through a well-organized convening of the Communist Party's Central Committee, were able to oust him in October 1964. This was the only time in Soviet history that a supreme leader had been removed; all the others died in office (Gorbachev was not removed by his peers; he lost his post when the USSR was dissolved in December 1991).

Khrushchev was initially replaced by an essentially bicephalous leadership team; heading the Communist Party was Leonid Brezhnev, while the state machinery was headed by Alexei Kosygin. The new leadership was determined to reverse the various failures for which Khrushchev had been blamed, and to overcome the humiliation he had brought to their country. By the end of the 1960s, most of the rest of the world had to acknowledge that the new Soviet leadership team had largely met its objectives. This could be seen in a number of ways.

First, the new team resolved to improve the country's economic performance. During 1965, two major reforms were introduced – one of agriculture, the other of industry and the economy more generally – designed to increase output and improve the quality of goods. While these policies eventually proved to be relative failures, initial results were encouraging.

Second, the new leadership clearly believed that there had been enough criticism of Stalin and the Stalin era. It was felt that this undermined the current system – which was, after all, essentially a product of Stalinism. While the new leadership did not return to the terror of the 1930s, they did substantially increase the level of state coercion over society. By the late 1960s, it was clear that the new Soviet leadership was intolerant of what they considered to be excessively liberal or critical artistic work. Solzhenitsyn's short novel had by now been banned, and censorship meant that none of his subsequent works could be published in the USSR. This intolerance had become very visible already by late 1965, with the arrests of Andrei Sinyavsky and Yuli Daniel for 'defamation of the Soviet system'; they had pseudonymously smuggled and published satirical manuscripts abroad. Following a short trial in early 1966, Sinyavsky and Daniel were sentenced respectively to seven and five years' detention in labour camps. This delivered a clear message that the relatively liberal artistic 'thaw' of the early 1960s was over. It also heralded the start of a policy of harassment of so-called dissidents in the USSR over the next few years.

Third, the Soviet leaders soon revealed that they would be at least as intolerant of challenges to Communism in states under Soviet domination as Khrushchev had proved to be in 1956. The clearest example of this was in their reaction to the so-called Prague Spring in 1968. This was another watershed in the history of Communist power, and deserves reasonably detailed consideration.

Unlike Hungary, and to a lesser extent Poland, Czechoslovakia had not experienced any liberalization after 1956. From the year of Stalin's death until January 1968, this central European state had been led by the hardline Communist Antonin Novotny. It is sometimes argued that most citizens in most types of political system will tolerate a reasonably authoritarian political system if that system delivers good economic performance. But the Czechoslovak economy had not been performing well in the 1960s, and pressure for reform had been increasing.

Contrary to what is commonly believed, the pressure for change within Czechoslovakia initially came not from the masses or even dissident intellectuals, but from the Communist party's own intelligentsia. Admittedly, a student strike in November 1967 about living conditions in university dormitories, and widespread criticism of the harsh way in which the police suppressed this demonstration, played a role in bringing the whole issue of Novotny's incompetent and increasingly arbitrary leadership into the political limelight. But this was only a trigger, the straw that broke the camel's back. A number of senior Communists had become increasingly critical of Novotny during 1967, and were quite open in their criticisms already from October, when a party debate on Czechoslovakia's trajectory was launched. Novotny realized his position was precarious, and appealed to the Soviets for support in the following month. In light of their own suppression of dissidents that was already underway, it might seem surprising that Moscow did not provide such support. But Moscow was loath to back a leader increasingly seen as a failure; when their treatment of Khrushchev is borne in mind, their position *vis-à-vis* Novotny looks more consistent.

Novotny was replaced as head of the party by Alexander Dubcek, head of the Slovak branch of the party. Dubcek was seen as a reformer, but a moderate one. At this point (early 1968), dissident intellectuals did start demanding more change. But it was still the party itself that was determining the pace and direction of change.

In April 1968, it published a new party programme – commonly known as the Action Programme – that advocated a number of political changes, including the introduction of a form of political pluralism and much greater religious freedom. While it still emphasized the leading role of the Communist party, the proposals raised expectations of real change. Despite warnings from conservative members that they were going too far, some of the more radical members of the Communist party published a document at the end of June that advocated much deeper change than had the April Action Programme. Trying to steer a middle course, Dubcek criticized aspects of the June manifesto (the *2000 Words*), particularly the call for strikes. Yet his comments were too weak for the more conservative members of the leadership, who criticized Dubcek and urged him to be firmer with the radicals.

But it was not only conservative Communist leaders in Prague who were becoming increasingly concerned about the direction in which their country was heading. Leaderships in neighbouring and nearby Communist states, particularly in East Berlin, Warsaw, and Moscow, were uneasy about the Czechoslovak developments, and in the middle of July published the 'Warsaw Letter' in most of the region's leading newspapers, in which they warned that developments in Czechoslovakia threatened socialism not only in that country, but also in surrounding ones.

The Warsaw Letter evoked mixed reactions in Czechoslovakia – anger at the fact that outsiders were interfering in the country's affairs, and trepidation that the Soviets might be gearing up for a repeat performance of Hungary 1956. From the time of the publication of the letter until mid-August, Dubcek and other members of the Czechoslovak leadership met with their Soviet and East European counterparts on a number of occasions, and assured them that they were not undermining socialism, either in their own country or anywhere else. Yet outsiders could see that there were mixed messages emanating from Prague. One of the clearest signs that Soviet-style Communist rule *was* being challenged was the publication in mid-August of a draft new party statute that contained some *very* radical proposals, including jettisoning one of the key components of Communist control, the *nomenklatura* list system. This system was designed to ensure that every important post in Czechoslovakia – in the political system, the educational system, the military, the media, the trade unions, and so on – was under the ultimate control of the Communist party, which had to be involved in one way or another in the hiring and firing of anybody to or from any post that was on the list.

The draft Communist party statute was the last straw for Communist leaders outside Czechoslovakia, who decided that their Czechoslovak comrades had to be brought into line. On 21 August 1968, troops from the USSR, Bulgaria, Hungary, and Poland entered Prague. Communists were once again invading a Communist state on the grounds that they had a duty to impose control over it for allegedly threatening the international Communist movement; this approach now became known as the Brezhnev Doctrine. But while there were some similarities with the invasion of Hungary in 1956, there were also important differences. One was that the invasion of Czechoslovakia involved troops from several Communist states (members of the Warsaw Pact); the Hungarian invasion had been by Soviet troops acting alone. Another significant difference was that, unlike the Hungarians, the Czechs and Slovaks put up little physical resistance. Sources differ on the number of people killed, but the range is between none and a little over 100; either way, the figure was dramatically lower than in Hungary. A final difference relates to the eventual outcome. Hungary's post-invasion leader proved over time to be increasingly liberal by Communist standards. Although there were attempts by the Soviets to reach a *modus vivendi* with the moderate reformers in the Czechoslovak system, including Dubcek, this eventually came to naught; by April 1969, Dubcek had resigned and been replaced by someone who proved to be a much more orthodox – conservative – Communist, Gustav Husak. Although Husak had originally (during mid-1968) expressed his support for Dubcek's position, he became increasingly hardline and intolerant once in power. The Prague Spring, and with it hopes for what Dubcek had called 'socialism with a human face', were history. Husak implemented a non-violent purge of the party – the so-called normalization – and Czechoslovakia was once again a strict Communist dictatorship.

A fourth and final way in which the more assertive stance of the post-Khrushchev Soviet leadership could be seen was in the build-up of the Soviet Union's military strength. The Brezhnev–Kosygin team was determined that the USSR would not be humiliated again in the way it had been over the Cuban Missile Crisis, and soon increased Soviet defence spending. By the end of the 1960s, the West had acknowledged that the USSR was now from many perspectives as powerful a military force as the USA. This point pertained not only to conventional force, but also to nuclear military power. If anyone had previously harboured any doubts, it was by now clear that the Soviet Union was a superpower, just like the USA.

One of the first Western politicians to acknowledge the superpower status of the USSR, and the dangers to world peace this could pose, was German Social Democrat Willi Brandt. He became German Chancellor (essentially, prime minister) in 1969, and almost immediately began to seek ways to improve relations with the Communist bloc, in line with his *Ostpolitik* (i.e. policy towards the East). Fortunately, he found Moscow to be responsive to his overtures, and relations between the West and the Communist world improved significantly in the first half of the 1970s. Although Stalinist and post-Stalin Soviet policy meant that the USSR had developed its heavy and defence industries to world-class standards, its light industries – particularly those oriented towards the consumer – were seriously lagging. The USSR was prepared to improve relations with the West in return for access to Western technology and know-how, especially in consumer-related fields.

Thus, while many in the West continued to criticize the USSR and several of its satellite states for their treatment of intellectual dissidents and striking workers, relations between the two major power blocs in the world improved substantially. This was the era of *détente* – the reduction of tension – between East and West. The two sides had been in a so-called Cold War since the late 1940s, and many hoped in the early 1970s that this was now drawing to a close and that a brighter less mutually hostile future lay ahead. The highpoint of *détente* came in 1975, when the West and the Soviet bloc signed the Helsinki Accords, as the major outcome of the CSCE (Conference on Security and Cooperation in Europe). This agreement was divided into three main sections or baskets – and within months, it became increasingly clear that the two sides had focused on different baskets. While both sides favoured that part of the first basket that focused on security, the Soviet bloc was in addition very interested in the second basket (concerning economic, scientific, and technological cooperation) and that part of the first basket that confirmed the existing borders within Europe. In contrast, the West was more interested in that part of the first basket that required both sides to respect human rights (Principle VII), and in the third, which focused on freedom to travel and of information. In other words, parts of the agreement were intended to address the concerns of those in the West and elsewhere who had criticized Western leaders for improving relations with countries that showed so little respect for the individual human rights of their citizens.

It soon became apparent that the Communist states had largely paid lip service to Principle VII and the third basket. In several of them, critical intellectuals set up Helsinki monitoring groups to track how their governments were performing in relation to human rights. One of the first was established in the USSR, under Yuri Orlov. But the Soviet authorities clamped down on this group, and by 1978 had tried and imprisoned many of its leading lights. Another example was Charter 77 in Czechoslovakia, established in 1977 to monitor the Czechoslovak government's record on human rights. Like their Soviet counterparts, the Czechoslovak authorities soon clamped down hard on this group, especially its leaders, including dissident playwright Vaclav Havel. At about the same time as these developments were occurring in the Communist world, the USA had elected a new president, Jimmy Carter, who had made the fight to respect human rights around the world one of his top priorities. Given all this, the *détente* of the early 1970s was soon replaced by a marked cooling of relations; the Cold War was back with a vengeance.

Major changes in Asia – and elsewhere

At roughly the same time as the new leadership team came to power in the USSR, Mao had begun to claw back his position in China. Having been sidelined to some extent in the early 1960s, he now made a renewed effort to become the undisputed senior leader again. It was in this situation that he unleashed the Great Proletarian Cultural Revolution (GPCR) – better known simply as the Cultural Revolution – in 1966; while the most extreme phase of this lasted until 1969, post-Mao Chinese historiography dates the ending of the Cultural Revolution as 1976, the year Mao died.

In many ways, the Cultural Revolution was the outcome of a power struggle, which in turn represented a clash of views on the best way to organize Chinese society. The two main approaches – the 'Two Lines' – were represented by Mao on the one hand, and Liu Shaoqi on the other. Mao maintained that China had become too bureaucratic and hierarchical, whereas Liu argued that it was necessary to have professionalism and hierarchy if the country was to progress in an orderly and efficient manner. Each of the Two Lines tended to attract different elements of the party and state machinery. Thus, the military and a new quasi-military group of young revolutionaries known as the Red Guards generally supported Mao, while Liu's base was more in the party and the state bureaucracy.

5. Red Guards support Mao during the Chinese Cultural Revolution

The Cultural Revolution wreaked havoc in China, and has been seen by post-Mao Chinese leaders as a serious mistake. At its height, people could be in trouble simply for listening to the 'wrong' type of music (e.g. European classical music, such as Beethoven) or reading 'bourgeois' literature. Like Soviet citizens in the 1930s, many ordinary Chinese citizens lived in fear of the authorities. But in some ways, the lot of those Chinese who survived was even worse than that of their Soviet counterparts. Educated Chinese could be accused of manifesting 'bourgeois' characteristics simply because of their better education levels – and if they were urban residents, there was a strong possibility that they would be forced to move to the countryside to work in the fields. According to the post-Mao Chinese authorities, almost 730,000 Chinese were directly persecuted during the GPCR, of whom almost 35,000 died as a direct result; some Western estimates suggest considerably higher numbers, with several million deaths. What is incontrovertible is that hundreds of millions of Chinese were seriously – negatively – affected in one way or another because of Mao's fanaticism and struggle for power. It was unquestionably one of the worst periods in Chinese Communist history, although the Great Leap Forward was responsible for even more deaths. Following Mao's death in September 1976, four senior leaders close to him, including his wife, were arrested; some four years later, this 'Gang of Four' was put on trial, and found guilty of having committed crimes against the Chinese people during the Cultural Revolution. Two of the four were sentenced to imprisonment, the other two to death (though this was subsequently commuted to life imprisonment). The trial of the Gang of Four was a show trial, and in one sense represented a continuation of the arbitrary coercion – the terror – of the Cultural Revolution. But at the same time, it also brought closure to that sorry phase of Chinese history.

Like other Communist states, China had no formal mechanisms for replacing a supreme leader, so that there was a power struggle following Mao's death. The principal contestants were the man Mao himself had proposed as his successor, Hua Guofeng – claimed by many to be Mao's illegitimate first son – and one who had suffered during the Cultural Revolution for being too 'bureaucratic' and 'pragmatic', Deng Xiaoping. By 1978, Deng was clearly in the ascendancy, and began what must really be seen as another revolution in China. This time, however, the revolution involved no terror or persecution. Rather, it was a revolution in the way the economy was managed, and started in the countryside. Deng was a firm believer in the need to unlock the entrepreneurial skills of the masses if China was to progress, and so encouraged a form of private initiative among the largest section of the population, the peasantry. For Deng, it was unimportant that others might criticize him for being too capitalist-oriented, as long as the lot of ordinary Chinese improved; as he expressed it in one of his most famous statements, 'It does not matter whether the cat is black or white; as long as it catches mice, it is a good cat.' His policies were, by almost any criteria, enormously successful, and laid the foundations for the economic powerhouse that China had become by the early 2000s.

During the 1970s, the Communists were also scoring successes elsewhere in Asia. Although Vietnam had come under Communist control in the mid-1940s, it was divided in 1954 following the ouster of the French colonial power; while the North remained Communist, the South became a republic in 1955, heavily oriented towards the West (especially the USA). But tensions between the two Vietnams increased, and by the 1960s they were at war. The USA supported South Vietnam in numerous ways, including militarily, and soon became directly involved in the Vietnam War. Unfortunately for them, both the South Vietnamese and the USA had seriously underestimated not merely the military skills but also the sheer determination of the North Vietnamese Communists. Under the political leadership of Ho Chi Minh (until his death in 1969) and then his successor Le Duan, and the military leadership of General Giap, North Vietnam proved to be a formidable enemy for the US, its allies (including Australia) and South Vietnam; by 1973, the US had conceded defeat. Two years later, the two Vietnams were reunited under Communist rule. At the same time, Communism spread to two of Vietnam's neighbours, Cambodia (also known as Kampuchea) and Laos. Communism was on the march again – and the West was licking its wounds.

If it was in Asia that Communism scored its major victory over the liberal capitalist West in the 1970s, it was also in Asia that Communism scored its *final* success over its arch-enemy – a victory that led to a new determination in the West to reassert itself over Communism. The events that led to this change focused on Afghanistan, which Soviet troops entered in December 1979. Contrary to popular belief, the Soviets did not go in to establish Communism; Afghanistan had already come under (local) Communist control in April 1978. Rather, the Soviets invaded Afghanistan to replace one type of Communist leader with another.

The original Communist leadership in Afghanistan had been hardline, yet had achieved little. It was thus becoming increasingly unpopular. This might not have been of any major consequence to the Soviets had it not been for other developments occurring in the region, notably in Iran. The latter oil-rich country had come under a new Islamic fundamentalist leader, Ayatollah Khomeini, in 1979, and was vehemently anti-Western. The Soviets apparently hoped that by installing a more moderate Communist leadership in Kabul, they could kill two birds with one stone. On the one hand, they could demonstrate to Muslims in neighbouring states that red and green – Communism and Islam – could co-exist; if this could be achieved, the USSR could hope for far more influence in the Middle East. On the other hand, if it could improve relations with various increasingly anti-Western Middle Eastern states, it could expect better access to the 'black gold' of the region, oil. This was the context in which the Soviets replaced the original Afghani Communist leadership (Taraki and Amin) with the much more moderate Karmal.

As mentioned above, the invasion of Afghanistan was the straw that broke the camel's back. The West had become increasingly concerned at the spread of Communism in the late 1960s and the 1970s – not only in Southeast Asia, but now also in Africa. Thus Communists and pro-Communist leadership teams had come to power in Congo (Brazzaville) in 1968, South Yemen in 1969, Benin in 1972, Ethiopia in 1974, and Angola and Mozambique in 1975. But by the beginning of the 1980s, leading Western nations had a new generation of much tougher-minded anti-Communist leaders, notably Margaret Thatcher in the UK (1979) and Ronald Reagan in the USA (1980). The tide was about to turn, and the days of Communist power's expansion were over.

Solidarity, Gorbachev, and communism's demise

Few would dispute that the most significant event in the history of Communism at the start of the 1980s was the emergence of

Solidarity in Poland. Of all the Soviet-oriented states, Poland had been the most troublesome over the years for the Communists; in addition to the troubles in 1956, there had been mass unrest there in 1968, 1970–1, and 1976. But, significant as they were, none of these periods of unrest could compare with what happened in 1980–1, when a new independent trade union – Solidarity – not only emerged and dwarfed the Polish Communist party in terms of membership, but was also formally recognized by the Communists as a legitimate organization until the declaration of martial law in December 1981.

As had so often been the case in the past, the initial trigger for the 1980 unrest was an economic one. In April, the Polish Communists had proposed removing subsidies on food; since Poles had little to thank their Communist leaders for other than subsidized food and housing, this proposal was a dangerous one. At the beginning of July, the subsidies were indeed removed on some items, and the price of meat in the shops attached to workplaces – where so many Poles usually bought their meat – increased 40 to 60%. Unlike in the past, Polish workers did not go on strike at this point; rather, they opted to elect their own representatives to negotiate with workplace managers for wage increases to compensate for the price rises. Surprisingly, the Polish authorities permitted such negotiations. However, it soon appeared that the authorities were hoping that the new arrangement would turn workers against workers, since those in enterprises with the most industrial muscle were able to negotiate much larger increases than others. But the Communists' policy backfired, as ever more workers made it clear that they were not prepared to allow the party to divide them through a policy of increasing inequality. As Polish workers realized what the authorities were doing – essentially pursuing a policy of divide and rule – so they began to go out on strike.

In the middle of August 1980, workers at the Lenin shipyard in Gdansk went on strike when the management sacked one of their leaders. The situation was escalating, and within days, workers not only in Gdansk but also in two neighbouring cities cooperated to produce a set of 21 demands to management and the Communist party. The workers also established an Inter-Factory Strike Committee, the seed from which Solidarity grew.

The Communists, under leader Edward Gierek, rejected the 21 demands, upon which the strikes spread across Poland. Gierek apparently decided at this stage to blame a scapegoat – so that he sacked the prime minister – and to pursue a policy of both carrot and stick to deal with a difficult situation that was rapidly escalating. Thus, at the same time as he recognized the right of the Inter-Factory Strike Committee to exist and negotiate with the government, he hinted that the Soviets might intervene and ordered the arrest of a number of the leading dissident intellectuals and workers. The latter approach – the stick – only inflamed the situation, and even more Polish workers went on strike. Although a majority of the Polish Politburo appears to have voted at this point to send in the military to end the strikes, Polish military chiefs warned the Communist leaders that they could not guarantee the loyalty of their troops, many of whom might side with the workers.

In this situation, the Polish Communists agreed to negotiate with the strikers' leaders, including the most famous of them, Lech Walesa. At the end of August, both sides signed the Gdansk Agreement. For a few days, Polish citizens were elated. But signs soon emerged that the authorities might be about to renege on this agreement. Symbolically, the most important indication of this was Gierek's resignation in early September and his replacement by the man who had been responsible since 1971 for security and the military, Stanislaw Kania. Faced with the possibility of a policy reversal, the workers' committees decided to dig their heels in; they were not about to be fobbed off yet again. Rather than capitulate, workers' leaders from around Poland met in late September to found Solidarity. The authorities now attempted further harassment of the striking workers, at which point Solidarity called

6. Lech Walesa, head of Poland's Solidarity (in 1980)

the first of what were to be many general strikes over the next fifteen months.

Solidarity continued to operate until December 1981. But by then, the Polish authorities' patience had run out. The new leader since October 1981, General Wojciech Jaruzelski, had held a meeting with Walesa and the head of the Polish Catholic church, Cardinal Glemp, in November to discuss the way forward. But the

Communists wanted Solidarity to cooperate with them in sorting out the economy, while Walesa insisted that Solidarity could only be involved in devising solutions to Poland's economic woes if a totally new body, independent of the Communist party (though involving members of it) were established. The failure of these talks, the increasing radicalism of Solidarity, and his awareness of growing unease among the Soviet and other East European Communist leaderships at Polish developments all combined to lead Jaruzelski to declare martial law in December 1981. Solidarity was now harassed even more than hitherto, though it was surely a sign of the confusion at the top of the Polish system that the trade union organization was not finally banned until October 1982. The imposition of this ban gave the Polish leadership more confidence that the situation was under control; martial law was suspended in December, and finally lifted altogether in July 1983.

By the time martial law was lifted in Poland, major developments were underway in the USSR. Leonid Brezhnev had died in office in November 1982. Although the Soviet Communists still had no formal leadership replacement mechanism, they had by this time learnt that prolonged leadership struggles were destabilizing, and a new leadership team was quickly and smoothly installed. This time, the former head of the KGB (security police), Yuri Andropov, became the new leader. Although he had had some modest plans for reform in the USSR, Andropov died within fifteen months before these could take effect and was replaced by the more conventional and rather dull Konstantin Chernenko. But his stint as leader was even shorter than Andropov's, since he died within some thirteen months of taking office. But if Andropov and/or Chernenko had been seen by the other senior Soviet leaders as caretakers, the man who took power in Moscow in March 1985 certainly was not. Ironically, that new General Secretary was the person seen by many commentators as the one who, more than any other individual, brought about the collapse of Communism. This was Mikhail Gorbachev, and he had a serious long-term reform agenda. He was also unlike any of his predecessors – more sophisticated, more willing to discuss, more broad-minded, less ideological; even arch-anti-Communist Margaret Thatcher had commented in December 1984 that she could 'do business' with this man!

Gorbachev came to power knowing that the USSR had serious problems, and soon set about addressing them. Above all, the Soviet economy was lagging. Back in 1961, the Communist Party of the Soviet Union had adopted a new Party Programme in which it was claimed that the USSR would overtake the USA in certain basics, such as meat consumption, by 1980. That objective was not met. Indeed, whereas the Soviet Union had enjoyed impressive economic growth rates up until the 1970s, these had slowed dramatically in the 1980s. Now the USSR was actually falling behind the West, let alone keeping pace, catching up with or even overtaking it. Gorbachev was very aware of this, and was determined to put Soviet economic development back on track. Thus he introduced a policy of restructuring (*perestroika*) that was intended to turn the economy around. However, Gorbachev soon realized that one of the major obstacles to economic reform was the central state bureaucracy, which had largely succeeded in blocking the implementation of major economic initiatives at least since Brezhnev and Kosygin had attempted to reform the economy back in 1965. Gorbachev believed that the most powerful weapon against a conservative, entrenched bureaucracy was the masses, so that he now adopted two further policies – *glasnost'* (openness) and *demokratizatsiya* (democratization). These encouraged ordinary citizens to speak openly about what was bothering them; Gorbachev hoped that their main target would be the bureaucrats.

Unfortunately, encouraging the masses to criticize the bureaucracy in Communist states could soon get out of hand – as Chinese leaderships had already discovered; Mao's 'Let a Hundred Flowers Bloom' campaign in 1956–7 and Deng's 'Democracy Wall' policy of 1978–9 had both resulted in far more criticism of the Communist system than the leadership had anticipated. But unlike Mao or

Deng, Gorbachev did not reassert central control when popular criticism went further than he would have preferred, and as the Soviet citizenry came to accept that the authorities were genuine this time in encouraging open debate, so the complaints came thick and fast. But they went far beyond just the contemporary bureaucracy; once the lid had been opened, almost any aspect of Soviet politics, history, and society became fair game for public debate. One of the most dangerous aspects of this venting of mass frustration was that nationalists in various parts of the Soviet Union took advantage of the new freedom to push for autonomy, and later independence.

Gorbachev was aware of what was happening, but hoped that improving the economy would placate most citizens. Moreover, he made clear his belief that ordinary Soviet consumers had suffered for too long not only because state bureaucracies had stymied economic reforms, but also because the USSR had overreached itself in trying to influence and assist other countries. By the late 1980s, therefore, he had withdrawn the Soviet troops from Afghanistan, and urged the Vietnamese Communists to leave Cambodia (which they had invaded in 1979).

Initially, Gorbachev's approach made him very popular, both at home and abroad. The withdrawal from Afghanistan was symbolically highly significant, since it was seen by many in the Communist world as a sign that, at last, the Soviets really would allow countries to go their own way; the Sinatra Doctrine (named after the American crooner's hit 'My Way') had replaced the Brezhnev Doctrine. When Gorbachev raised no objections to Hungarian and Polish proposals to introduce a form of pluralism into their systems, citizens throughout most of Communist Eastern Europe began to believe that they would at last be able to challenge their own Communist governments without having to fear a Soviet or Warsaw Pact invasion. One by one, starting with Hungary and Poland in 1989, the Communist systems of Eastern Europe collapsed. The last to fall were those in which the local

Communists had taken power themselves – Albania, Yugoslavia, and the USSR itself. But by the end of 1991, even these states had overthrown Communist power. Not only this, but the USSR finally and formally disintegrated in December 1991, while a similar – if more protracted and bloody – process was also underway in Yugoslavia. The Communists also lost power at this time in Afghanistan, Cambodia, Mongolia, and elsewhere. With notable exceptions in East Asia and the Caribbean (Cuba), Communist power had been overthrown. And even in some of those countries in which the Communists retained power, there were clear signs of crisis at this time. The best example was China, where the Communists had to use military force in June 1989 to suppress demonstrators in Tiananmen Square. Protesters there and elsewhere in Beijing and other major cities (e.g. Shanghai) had for weeks been calling for greater democracy and less corruption. But the majority of the Chinese leadership was in no mood to make concessions, and used force to end the unrest. According to the Chinese authorities, some 200 to 300 people lost their lives as a result; but many unofficial sources claim the figure was 2,000 to 3,000. Communist power globally had thus, depending on the country, either collapsed or else once again shown its uglier – coercive – side.

Chapter 3
The political system of communism

On one level, the political system of Communism was relatively simple, in that all Communist states were *de facto* one-party states. However, on another level they had complicated political systems, at least from the perspective of someone used to a Western one. The main reason for this complexity was that there was in fact a dual structure. As the vanguard, the Communist party was to play the 'leading role' in the political system, while the state was responsible for passing laws and implementing these. Unfortunately, the party often in practice duplicated the roles that were supposed to be the responsibility of the state, resulting in a confused and opaque political process. While Communist leaderships were often aware of this, and warned against the party duplicating or substituting itself for the state, practice was often less clear cut than the theory of a division of labour between the party and state. For this reason, it is appropriate to refer to Communist systems as party–state complexes.

The party

Given that Communist systems were often described in Western media as 'one-party states', it comes as a surprise to many to learn that several Communist states *formally* had (in the case of those still in existence, have) multi-party systems. Among those Communist states with several political parties were Bulgaria,

Czechoslovakia, East Germany, and Poland – while China, North Korea, and Vietnam continue to permit minor parties. However, it would be quite wrong to see these minor parties as opposition parties, since they were never allowed to challenge the Communist party's position. It is therefore better to call even the formally multi-party systems one-party than dominant-party, since the latter could be applied to countries with very different systems (e.g. Japan, India, and Italy for much of their recent histories). The minor parties were permitted to exist for several reasons; these included historical ones, the Communists' desire to keep an eye on potential dissidents, and as a defence against charges that their country was not democratic. On the last point, it is noteworthy that most of the Communist states that were traditionally parts of a larger country (i.e. China, East Germany, North Korea, North Vietnam) *formally* had multi-party systems; the Communists sought to counter anti-Communist propaganda from their capitalist counterparts by claiming to have socialist democracy and a multi-party system. The only exception to this point about divided countries was South Yemen, which was a one-party state. But given the strict subordination of the minor parties to the Communists in *all* Communist states, it is appropriate to refer even to those countries that permitted or permit minor parties as one-party states, as long as it is borne in mind that the formal arrangement can be subtly different across countries.

Just as some Communist countries formally had multi-party systems while others were unambiguously one-party states, so the party was actually called a Communist party (e.g. the Communist Party of the Soviet Union; the Chinese Communist Party; the Communist Party of Cuba) in some countries, but not in others. What was in fact the Communist party was called the Socialist Unity Party in East Germany, the Kampuchean People's Revolutionary Party in Cambodia, and the Polish United Workers' Party in Poland, for example. Historical reasons usually explained this. Thus, if the word 'united' appeared in the title, this generally indicated that the Communists had formed an alliance with socialists or other left-wing parties in the early days of the new regime. In the particular case of Yugoslavia – where the party was called the League of Communists – it was not the absence of the term 'communist', but rather 'party', that deserves comment. Once the Yugoslavs became estranged from Moscow in the late 1940s, they sought to distance themselves from the Soviet model, and believed that the term 'League' (adopted in 1952) was more in line with Marx's principles, whereas the word 'Party' was more associated with Lenin. The Yugoslav decision was thus meant to symbolize that Yugoslavia was pursuing a more genuinely Marxist model than the Leninist one adopted by the Soviets.

Despite their different names, Communist parties were all structured according to the principle of democratic centralism. It is important to note which is the noun and which the modifier here; the term stood for a form of centralism, not a type of democracy. In the last (1986) Party Statute of the Communist Party of the Soviet Union, democratic centralism was defined as follows:

A. Election of all leading Party bodies, from the lowest to the highest;
B. Periodic reports of Party bodies to their Party organizations and to higher bodies;
C. Strict Party discipline and subordination of the minority to the majority;
D. The decisions of higher bodies are unconditionally binding on lower bodies;
E. Collectivity in the work of all organizations and leading organs of the party and personal responsibility of every Communist for the fulfilment of his or her duties and party assignments.

In practice, this set of principles meant that the centre took all the important decisions, which lower levels of the party were then to accept and implement unquestioningly.

The structure of Communist parties varied somewhat from country to country, depending on factors such as the size of the population and whether or not the country was federal. However, the basic logic of the structure was common and pyramidal. At the lowest level – that at which a person joined – was the primary or base (the name depending on the country) party organization. Above this were local, district, regional, and sometimes provincial or republic-level party organizations. At the central level, there were four main bodies – the Party Congress; the Central Committee; the Secretariat; and the Politburo.

The Party Congress was a large body – most had memberships in the thousands – that typically met only once every five or so years for a few days. Its tasks included approving the reports from smaller central bodies about how the country had progressed since the previous Congress; formally deciding on the general direction of the party and country over the next quinquennium; and electing the Central Committee. In practice, the members of the Congress were usually told who to vote for; this was not a body that challenged the smaller central agencies.

The Central Committee was much smaller than the Congress, typically numbering a few hundred members. It usually met twice a year on average, and for a day or two at a time. At these sessions, the Central Committee would discuss either a specific topic – perhaps the economy or foreign policy or education – or else a range of issues. The Central Committee was also responsible for electing the real centres of power in any Communist system, the Secretariat and the Politburo.

On one level, the Secretariat normally played the role that might be expected of a secretariat in any kind of system. Thus it would prepare agendas for and provide information to the supreme decision-making body, the Politburo. Like any body that prepares agendas and provides information, the Secretariat enjoyed considerable power to influence decisions – both in recommending what issues were discussed by the Politburo and in deciding what information was provided to assist the Politburo members to reach their decisions. Indeed, it is testimony to the enormous power of the average party Secretariat that the person who was in almost any Communist system *the* leader was the First or General (the terms are essentially interchangeable) Secretary. Endorsing the point made above concerning substitution and duplication, many secretariats were structured in such a way that secretaries 'shadowed' one or more ministers in the state machinery. One other task primarily performed by the Secretariat – administration of the *nomenklatura* system – will be considered below, since it was sufficiently important to deserve consideration in its own right. For now, the focus turns to the political heart of any Communist system, the Politburo.

Politburos were small bodies – usually between 10 and 25 members, depending on the country and period, and whether or not one includes only full (voting) members or also candidate (non-voting) members. Typically, they would meet once a week, or sometimes once a fortnight, and would make all the most important decisions for society. The *de facto* head of the Politburo, the General or First Secretary, was the supreme leader in any Communist system; often, he – it was never a she – would be either the head of state and/or the head of the government at the same time as he headed the Communist party.

The structures of the party were designed to facilitate the implementation of a number of functions. One of the party's primary tasks was to set goals for society. In theory, it was the party's task to set long-term goals, such as industrialization or Communism. Increasingly, as the years went by, leaderships tended to focus more on short- and medium-term goals, such as the economic plan for the next year or the next five years.

But the party was also responsible for ensuring that the goals it set were reached – goal attainment. The party's role in this was supposed to be largely supervisory, ensuring that state bodies implemented the tasks the party had set. In practice, however,

Communism

7. The Soviet Politburo (1977)

there was often overlap between party and state bodies; but party leaders' warnings against the dangers of substitution were all too often made half-heartedly or fell on deaf ears. After all, many party functionaries were keen to exercise as much power as possible.

A third function of Communist parties was to socialize the population, so that citizens knew where society was heading and why, and would accept the party's right to rule. The party's need to explain and justify its actions became increasingly important over time, as most leaderships moved away from the overt terror of the Stalinist era in the USSR, or the immediate post-World War II years in Eastern Europe, or the Cultural Revolution in China. The party sought to socialize the population in various ways. This included control of the educational system, control of the mass media, and direct communication with the citizenry during election campaigns. In this context, it is worth noting that the term propaganda usually had a positive connotation for Communists.

The fourth function of the party – recruitment – was arguably *the* most powerful weapon in the party's armoury for controlling society. This power was exercised above all through the *nomenklatura* system, an understanding of which is vital if one is to grasp how Communists kept control over society. The *nomenklatura* was a secret list kept by the Secretariats at each level of the party, and included all the posts at that administrative level considered important by the party. The list included not only positions within the party, but also in councils, enterprises, educational establishments, the police force, the trade unions, women's organizations, youth organizations, the media (both print and electronic), the military, and elsewhere. The party was to be directly involved in hiring individuals to or firing them from what were identified as the most important posts on the *nomenklatura*, and was to be kept informed about such hiring and firing in the case of posts considered of secondary significance. While certain realities – such as the absence of limitless pools of appropriate people for any given position – mean that the party did not have an *unlimited* capacity to place whoever it wanted in any important post in society, the *nomenklatura* system did provide it with enormous power to move people in and out of key positions virtually at will. The *nomenklatura* system was the party's trump card.

A final function of the party was to create linkages between itself and society. While the numerous examples of mass unrest reveal that this linkage function was not always performed well, most Communist parties considered it important to develop these ties, in part to keep their finger on society's pulse and thus, they hoped, to pre-empt major outbursts of discontent.

It is an irony of history that parties committed to the eventual emergence of highly egalitarian societies were in many ways among the most elitist in the world. Not only were Communists intolerant of other parties – either banning them altogether as in the USSR or Romania, or else keeping them under strict control (i.e. in those Communist states that formally permitted a multi-party system) – but they also adopted an exclusive approach to party membership. This conundrum becomes easier to understand if Lenin's notion of the Communist party as the 'vanguard' is recalled. The party was never to include just anyone who wanted to join, but rather was to comprise the politically most aware members of society, those who best understood the logic of history and who would devote themselves to the achievement of first socialism and then communism. It is therefore unsurprising that the membership of Communist parties never exceeded a relatively small percentage of the population, as revealed in Table 1.

Several points emerge from Table 1. First, even in countries in which the membership of the party was the highest in the Communist world, the percentage was still small compared with the total population; unfortunately, lack of appropriate data for several countries means that it is not possible to produce a table based solely on adult population, which would be preferable. Second, there was a general if unsurprising tendency for the newer Communist states – in Africa and Southeast Asia – to have had much lower membership rates than the more established ones, though it is noteworthy that the oldest Communist states, the USSR and Mongolia, were not among those with the highest membership rates. Third, the general tendency was for the more economically developed states to have had higher membership rates than the less developed ones. Finally, and counterintuitively, countries that tolerated parties other than the Communist party did not as a result have lower average Communist party membership levels than countries in which the Communist party was the only one; in fact, the opposite was generally true.

A concluding point about Communist parties relates to Milovan Djilas' claim that they constituted ruling classes. In that Communist parties did control society, the term ruling is unexceptionable. But since the classical Marxist notion of class is based on ownership (property), the term ruling *class* is on balance an inappropriate one for Communist systems. On the one hand,

Table 1. Membership of the party as a percentage of the total population (early 1980s) and nature of party system

Rank	Country	Percentage	Formal multi-party system?
1	North Korea	16.0	Yes
2	Romania	14.6	No
3	East Germany	13.1	Yes
4	Czechoslovakia	10.4	Yes
5	Bulgaria	9.7	Yes
6	Yugoslavia	9.6	No
7	Hungary	8.0	No
8	Soviet Union	6.7	No
9	Poland	6.3	Yes
10=	Albania	4.4	No
10=	Cuba	4.4	No
12	Mongolia	4.2	No
13	China	4.0	Yes
14	Vietnam	3.0	Yes
15	Laos	1.0	No
16	(South Yemen)	0.9	No
17	(Mozambique)	0.8	No
18	Afghanistan	0.6	No
19=	(Angola)	0.4	No
19=	(Congo)	0.4	No
21	Cambodia	0.01	No
22	(Ethiopia)	0.006	No
23	(Benin)	0.005	No

Note: Bracketed countries are those whose status as Communist is disputed.

the Communists' control of the means of production can be used as the basis for arguing that they constituted a class. On the other hand, while senior Communists were typically wealthier than average citizens and had access to many perks, they did not formally own the means of production. Moreover, and with some notable exceptions, nor were they generally able to transmit their privileges to their children. At the most, the term ruling class should only be applied – if at all – to the senior *apparatchiks* (i.e. full-time professional party functionaries). It would be unjustified to claim that the entire membership of a party constituted a ruling class.

The state

If the Communist party was to guide or lead society, the tasks of the state in Communist countries included passing and implementing laws, interpreting and applying those laws, and defending the country. It thus comprised the legislature, ministries, local councils, the courts, the police (including the secret police), and the military.

The legislatures in the Communist world were mostly unicameral (i.e. a single house); the only exceptions to this were the three federal Communist states (Czechoslovakia, Soviet Union, Yugoslavia), which had both Lower and Upper Houses. Most legislatures were called the National or People's Assembly; exceptions include the Supreme Soviet (literally, Council) in the USSR and the National People's Congress in China. Some commentators have described Communist legislatures as parliaments, but this is in almost all cases misleading. The term 'parliament' derives from an Old French word for to talk or speak, and in the English language usually implies a national political space in which discussions take place, as well as a legislature. But Lenin's ban on factionalism within the Communist party was soon expanded into state structures, and free discussion was not generally a feature of Communist legislatures; rare exceptions

8. The Chinese National People's Congress

included Yugoslavia and Poland on occasions. Another exception that proves the rule is provided by the East German legislature. In its 40-year history, the People's Chamber only once experienced a less than unanimous vote; this was in 1972, when the East German Communists permitted members of the Christian Democratic Union a conscience vote on the proposed new abortion law. But this vote in no way threatened the Communists' position or represented open opposition; the whole process was tightly controlled.

In some ways, ministries in Communist states were not dissimilar to their counterparts in Western systems. Thus there were ministries dealing with foreign affairs, internal affairs, foreign trade, education, and so on. But there were also important differences. First, since Communists in general believed not in market economics but in state control of the economy, there were far more ministries dealing with economic issues than there are in capitalist systems. Not only were there ministries for each sector and branch of an economy, but often even for sub-branches (e.g. various types of engineering in the USSR). Moreover, since most

Communists placed great emphasis on the need to have economic plans for future development, there was a state planning agency, equivalent to a super-ministry. A second difference from *some* Western states (e.g. the UK, but not West Germany) was that ministerial officials in Communist states were supposed to be overtly loyal to (and usually members of) the ruling party; the notion that such officials might seek – let alone be expected – to maintain a certain distance from their political masters was anathema in Communist systems.

Even highly centralized systems cannot administer everything from the capital; this becomes even more obvious in huge countries like the USSR or China. Thus Communist states had local administrations. But the power of these varied considerably according to time and place. At least in theory, the country in which they had the most power was Yugoslavia, with its self-management system. In recent years, Chinese local organs' powers have also increased significantly.

A key aspect of the rule of law is that the courts should be able to enjoy a high degree of independence from the more overtly partisan elements of the political system. No such expectation existed in Communist systems. The primary loyalty expected of courts was to the Communist system, not to the law. In practice, those brought before the courts were in most states usually assumed to be guilty, not innocent. And the notion that citizens would be able to appeal to a supreme court against unfair treatment by 'the system' was virtually unknown.

Police forces in most Communist states were divided into the regular police and the security or secret police. The former dealt with non-political crimes, while the latter was more concerned with intelligence concerning state security. In practice, this meant that the security police – such as the KGB in the USSR, the *Stasi* in East Germany, the *Securitate* in Romania, or the *Guoanbu* in China – were often perceived as a police force focused heavily on alleged political dissidence. The heads of the security police were typically very powerful, often having a seat on the Politburo: in fact, former head of the KGB Yuri Andropov rose to become the USSR's supreme leader.

The military also played an important political role in Communist states, in addition to its more conventional role of defending the country; again, its head would often be a member of the Politburo. One indication of the significance of the military in some Communist states is the fact that senior military leaders occasionally became a country's supreme leader, such as General Jaruzelski in Poland. In addition, civilian leaders often had themselves appointed Commander-in-Chief of the Armed Forces; a good example was Cuba's Fidel Castro, who usually appeared in public in military uniform. In some states, the military sometimes performed general administrative tasks and assisted with urgent tasks, such as harvesting, when this was deemed necessary. This was particularly true of Maoist China and the early years of the Cuban Communist system. Communist militaries were typically structured along similar hierarchical lines to their Western counterparts, although China temporarily abolished the distinction between officers and ordinary soldiers during the Cultural Revolution. Conscription was obligatory, though some Communist states, such as East Germany, permitted social service for conscientious objectors. A final important point is that although the military was usually a very loyal component of any Communist system, senior military officers did occasionally challenge and even plot against their Communist civilian leaders; prime examples include Albania in 1960, Bulgaria in 1965, and the USSR in 1991.

Elections

Given the essentially one-party and centrally directed nature of Communist systems, it might seem incongruous that they had elections. In order to understand the purpose of these, it is necessary to jettison Western notions of an election as an activity designed primarily to give voters a choice of candidates and parties for political office. Although several Communist states began to introduce elements of choice into their elections in the 1980s (some, such as Hungary, had begun in a limited way even earlier), this was still ultimately under the control of the Communist party in the vast majority of cases. Thus even non-Communist candidates would almost always have been carefully scrutinized by the Communists before being permitted to run for office. Moreover, since the Communists usually had (unacknowledged) quotas for representation in national legislatures – by gender, class, ethnicity – there were severe structural constraints on electoral freedom anyway.

So what was the point of Communist elections? First, several Communist states saw no problem in allowing voters a limited (i.e. non-threatening) choice. Such choice as did exist was usually between types of personality – for example, between a younger, more dynamic but less experienced candidate and an older, less dynamic but more experienced and better-known one. Thus, voters did have an opportunity to express mildly conflicting preferences in some Communist states, albeit usually more so in local than in national elections. Moreover, some Communist states had turnover requirements, meaning that a certain percentage of parliamentarians or local councillors had to be replaced on a regular basis; elections were a way of achieving this that looked reasonably democratic. Second, elections were a channel through which Communists could communicate with the population. Especially during the nomination and pre-election phases, Communist officials would explain new policies, justify the party-state complex's actions directly to the public – and sometimes listen to complaints (again, much more so in the context of local than of national elections). Third, it must be remembered that the vast majority of Communist states had experienced little or no real democracy before the Communists took power, so that citizen experiences and expectations were different from those of citizens in established liberal democracies; the only significant exception to this point was Czechoslovakia, which had been a flourishing democracy in the inter-war period. *Some* Communists were genuine in their belief that elections were a way of educating the mass population about political participation, even if this process was carefully controlled. Finally, elections were intended to assist in the legitimation of Communist systems – both to their own populations, and as a way of making it more difficult for anti-Communists in other countries to claim there was no democracy in Communist systems.

With the exception of Cambodia, voting was not formally compulsory in Communist states. However, many citizens believed they would suffer in some way – perhaps when they applied for a job promotion, or when their children applied for a university place – if they did not cast their vote. Whether or not this was an accurate perception, it helps to explain why voter turnout in Communist states was exceptionally high, particularly in national elections. Arguably the most liberal Communist state, Yugoslavia, tended to have the lowest turnouts; but even these were usually above 90%, while the rate was above 98% in most countries, and almost 100% in Albania and North Korea.

Electoral methods varied across the Communist world, with both direct and indirect systems, and both single- and multi-member constituencies. Although many Communist states claimed that their elections were secret, most were not in any meaningful sense. Thus many citizens believed that if they were to enter a polling booth, this would be seen as a potential form of dissent, and so would drop their ballot forms into the ballot box unmarked – in this way demonstrating their acceptance of the candidate or candidates proposed by the electoral authorities.

While moves towards greater electoral choice in some Communist states by the 1980s were welcome, their significance should not be exaggerated. After all, national elections were for deputies to legislatures that rarely witnessed real debate. Moreover, all state agencies were officially subordinate to the Communist party anyway, and ordinary voters had no say over who their Communist leaders would be.

Civil society

So far, the focus in this chapter has been on the formal political institutions of the party–state complex. But what of other aspects of politics, in particular the political role that can be played by civil society?

Unless a very minimalist approach to democracy is adopted – one that sees it as being little more than a system ensuring regular, free, and genuinely contested elections – civil society is a key element of a real democracy. Unfortunately, the meaning of the term is highly contested. Here, civil society refers to a situation in which citizens can organize themselves more or less independently of the state, whether this be for the purposes of business and trade, religion, sport, the exchange of information, or any other activity. Two key features of a genuine civil society are that it organizes itself (i.e. it is not managed by the state), and that its existence is recognized – considered legitimate – by the state. In the absence of either or both of these variables, there is no real civil society. While citizens in most Communist states were frequently mobilized for marches and other activities, these were typically organized by the state. Hence such activity did not constitute civil society. While religion was only ever *formally* banned in one Communist state (Albania 1967), it was strongly discouraged in most cases; this too indicates the absence of civil society. As for the free exchange of information – the media in most Communist states were very much under state control, once again indicating the absence of civil society. And while Poland's Solidarity is sometimes taken as evidence of the existence of genuine civil society in a Communist state, the fact that it was banned for several years in the 1980s means that our second criterion (full recognition by the state) was not met. The various examples of mass unrest, when citizens did challenge their Communist authorities, should be seen not as evidence of civil society, but rather as protest politics.

Were communist states totalitarian?

Totalitarianism was a popular term in the 1950s and 1960s for describing both fascist and Communist systems. Following the collapse of Communist power, it became popular again, as many commentators from formerly Communist systems described their previous systems as totalitarian. But how useful and appropriate is this term? Does it make sense to use the same word to describe Stalin's USSR at the height of the 1930s Terror or Pol Pot's Cambodia in the 1970s with the relatively easy-going Hungary or Yugoslavia of the 1980s, or even Khrushchev's USSR of the late 1950s and early 1960s?

The best-known exposition of totalitarianism remains that of Carl Friedrich and Zbigniew Brzezinski in their 1956 book *Totalitarian Dictatorship and Autocracy*. In this, they identify six salient features of a totalitarian system that can be summarized as a single chiliastic (i.e. geared towards long-term peace and happiness) ideology; a single mass party, typically led by a dictator; state terror; a near monopoly of mass communications; a near monopoly of weapons; and a centrally planned economy. It should be obvious that a number of these features applied to Communist systems. However, the *extent* to which they applied varied by time and place. It is therefore advisable to adopt a relativistic approach when using the term 'totalitarian'. In other words, we can say that Country A was more totalitarian in the 1950s than it was in the 1980s, but still more totalitarian in the 1980s than Country B was.

Chapter 4
The economic system of communism

One of the clearest distinctions between Western systems and Communist ones was in how their economies functioned. To understand these differences, it is necessary briefly to consider how Western systems operate. Despite sometimes significant variations, all Western systems were (and remain) basically capitalist. Two of the main features of capitalist systems have been a predominance of private ownership and a broad commitment to letting the market rather than the state determine prices. This is not to suggest that there was no state ownership or state control of prices in capitalist systems; nationalization of parts of the economy was common in many West European countries after World War II, while such states also typically determined prices for citizens' basic needs, such as water and other utilities, and provided many collective goods, such as subsidized public transport.

There were also major differences in the amount and type of state involvement Western countries opted for. Some believed that the best way in which a state could and should interfere in the economy, particularly when the latter was experiencing major problems such as no or negative growth, was for the government to kick-start it by commissioning large-scale projects, typically infrastructural ones such as major highways or new airports. The logic behind this was that such projects would then have positive knock-on effects elsewhere in the economy, which in turn would start to grow again. This version of capitalism is often called Keynesianism, after the British economist John Maynard Keynes who theorized and advocated it in the 1930s. While popular for only a brief period in the 1930s in the USA (in the form of President Roosevelt's 'New Deal'), the approach was popular in much of Western Europe for two to three decades after the end of World War II.

But starting in the 1970s, a more rugged – less state-dependent – form of capitalism began to spread in the West. This was neo-liberalism, and was associated with Western politicians such as Margaret Thatcher (UK) and Helmut Kohl (Germany), as well as economic theorists such as Milton Friedman and Friedrich Hayek. In this approach, the state leaves much more to the market than it does in the Keynesian version of capitalism. If the economy encounters serious problems, the state seeks to solve these not through funding major new projects, but through reducing interest rates. The thinking behind this approach is that if capital is cheap to borrow, entrepreneurs and investors will borrow money from banks and other lenders to invest in new or upgraded projects, thus stimulating the economy to grow.

But, at least until their final days, Communist governments in Eastern Europe and the USSR adopted neither of these capitalist approaches. They maintained that leaving pricing to the market was anarchic, while encouraging private ownership of the means of production, particularly large-scale industrial production, was immoral and outdated.

Types of ownership

In Communist states, most factories, banks, and other forms of enterprise were owned by the state. Communists called this *social ownership* of the means of production. Most Westerners are more familiar with the term *nationalized*; this is an acceptable term to use, as long as it is understood that different levels of the state (centre, republic, local municipality, etc.) in Communist systems could own economic enterprises. There were occasional exceptions to this notion of social ownership, with the last privately owned factory in East Germany – a perfume factory! – being nationalized as late as 1972.

Ownership in the countryside was more complex. Some farms were completely owned by the state, and hence were called *state* farms; the people working on these had similar conditions to their counterparts working in factories. Thus, they received guaranteed minimum incomes, irrespective of natural conditions (e.g. changing weather conditions from year to year), and were entitled to state pensions. A second type of arrangement was the *collective* farm. Their original development in the USSR was in line with Stalin's approach to the modernization of the Soviet economy. His commitment to the concept is reflected in the scale and pace of their development; between 1928 and 1931, the number of collective farms increased from 33,300 to 211,100, while the percentage of peasant households collectivized rose dramatically, from 1.7% to 52.7%. Whereas the state owned the land in collective farms, the machinery, buildings, seeds, animals, and so on belonged collectively to those who worked the land, the collective farmers. The conditions of collective farmers were usually different from those of their peers in state farms. Their income was more variable, subject *inter alia* to the whims of the weather, and many were not guaranteed state retirement pensions; it was not until the 1960s that Soviet collective farmers became eligible for such pensions, for example.

One feature common to most state and collective farmers was that they were both entitled to small *private* plots; Albania was an exception, and did not permit such plots. Farmers were permitted to grow food or raise animals on their plots for personal consumption, but were also free to sell any excesses in private markets. Had it not been for these private markets, urban dwellers in many Communist countries would have found it much more

9. Early days of Soviet collectivization (1929)

difficult to buy eggs, chickens, rabbits, and other types of food; Poland and Yugoslavia took private ownership in the countryside even further, in that most farms in these two states were privately owned and operated.

The small private plots and the related private food markets were not the only form of private enterprise, however. Again with the notable exception of hardline Albania, where citizens were not even permitted to purchase private cars, most Communist states were by the 1970s allowing small-scale private enterprise in urban areas too. There were a small number of private shops, restaurants, taxis, and tradespeople in many Communist states in the later years of Communist power. The general guideline was that these private enterprises should not be large enough to require many staff, off whose labour the entrepreneur could live without working. This approach was said to be compatible with Marxism, since it did not permit the emergence of large-scale capitalism or exploitation.

A number of Communist states also permitted *cooperative* ownership of housing. Here, a group of citizens would pool resources to build a (usually small) apartment block, into which they would move. Again, the Communist justification of this was that people were acting together – communally – to help themselves, rather than to generate capital and exploit others.

All of the forms of ownership described so far were legal and open. But there was always also an informal – unregistered and unrecorded – private economy, parts of which were illegal. Sometimes, this involved actual payment to a tradesperson or someone else who was offering their services clandestinely. But at other times, a form of bartering operated. A plumber might be prepared to offer his services to a farmer in return for a chicken, for example. Such shadow economy activity did not show up in any official economic statistics.

Central planning

His belief that markets were anarchic and that socialist systems should be planned led Lenin to establish a planning agency in Russia in 1921. But central planning in the USSR then went on hold for most of the 1920s, as the NEP kick-started the economy again after World War I and the Civil War. By the late 1920s, having consolidated power, Stalin revisited the issue of planning, and decided that a centrally planned economy (hereafter CPE) was now both possible and desirable. Stalin considered such a system the most efficient way to develop the Soviet economy quickly into a predominantly urban and industrial one – i.e. the type Marx considered a vital precondition for a genuinely socialist system – and therefore introduced the USSR's first five-year plan in 1928. From then on, the Soviet economy operated according to economic plans (mostly, though not exclusively, five-year ones). While the plan was initially oriented towards industry, Stalin soon decided that it could not function properly if agriculture were excluded, so that the latter was incorporated.

As Communist power spread after World War II, so the economies of Communist Eastern Europe and Asia became CPEs. In most cases, the plans were highly directive; although production units were supposed to have some say in their future plans, in practice this right was usually very limited. This was not only because of the natural tendency of most Communist systems to centralism, but also because only the centre was in a position to coordinate the plans of thousands of units. In short, typically the centre ultimately decided the plans, and enterprises and other economic units were expected to fulfil them. A notable exception to this general pattern was Yugoslavia. In line with its commitment to 'self-management', it granted broader decision-making powers to production units than was typical in other Communist countries. Its plans were far less restrictive, and increasingly indicative rather than directive. In recent years, China has moved to a 'dual track' approach, attempting to mix both planning and market principles in what is sometimes an uneasy combination.

Communists claimed that CPEs had several advantages over market economies. One was that they permitted conscious steering of the economy in whichever direction was considered most beneficial, and for rational distribution and prioritization – by sector, branch, region, class, and ethnicity. Another claimed advantage was that CPEs could produce stable, fair, and rational prices, based more on the cost of inputs (including labour) and use value than on what Communists saw as the whims of the market. Marx had criticized the dominant form of pricing in capitalist systems, namely the tendency for prices to reflect the balance between the availability of a good or service (plus profits) and the demand for it, in what market economists call equilibrium theory. In his view, the real value of an item was the amount of labour that went into producing it and its usefulness; most Communist systems claimed to have adopted pricing policies that were more or less in line with this approach to value. A third putative advantage was that CPEs were able to resist external pressures, including from what is nowadays called globalization. A final claimed benefit of CPEs was that they were able to ensure full employment.

But in practice, while CPEs were able to secure some of these advantages – the prices of many basic goods were often low, and stable for long periods; unemployment as usually understood in the West was very uncommon – they also suffered from a number of disadvantages. One was that in reality, groups had unequal power to pursue their interests in most Communist systems. Thus the so-called steel-eaters (the military and heavy industry) had more influence in the Soviet system than light industry had, which usually ensured there were enough tanks and guns, but did not prevent severe shortages of consumer goods. This meant in turn that many Communist economies were skewed (i.e. imbalanced), with some sectors well developed and others very under-developed. Attempts to redress this imbalance from the 1960s on were at best only partly successful.

Another problem was that the production of plans became ever more difficult over time as economies became increasingly complex. This encouraged a conservative or incremental approach in planning – simply tinkering at the margins because it was too difficult to do otherwise. This tinkering reflected what planners and economists sometimes call the ratchet effect.

Arising from the previous point, CPEs in practice experienced increasing problems of innovation. The introduction of new equipment, techniques, and ideas became more difficult, because of the problems involved in coordinating this with existing production.

A fourth problem was that prices were in an important sense distorted, since they did not *per se* send messages about over- or under-supply – i.e. about what was actually needed. Much pricing in Communist economies was far from rational; it was not to any meaningful extent based on the cost of labour or usefulness, nor did it tell producers what was needed.

Similarly, the quality of goods was often poor because prices were not sending appropriate messages. Quality could also be affected by the problem of 'storming'; given that production was largely dictated by plans and workers had too little incentive to work hard, factories would often work at a leisurely pace for much of a month or plan period, and then operate at a furious pace to ensure fulfilment of the plan – often with negative effects on the quality of the goods produced.

The point about too few incentives to work harder and more efficiently requires explanation. The combination of inexpensive basics – housing, utilities, public transport, etc. – and a poor supply of high-quality consumer goods meant that there was little incentive for workers to work harder (i.e. because there was little they wanted to or could buy), which in turn had a negative effect on labour productivity.

While full or nearly full employment might be seen as socially desirable, it often resulted in labour market distortions. Harsh as this might be on individuals, dynamic economies need flexible workforces, so that excessively secure workplace arrangements can work against the long-term interests of society. The fact that Communist economies sometimes experienced labour shortages in some sectors and branches while workers were underemployed or engaged in tedious work in others endorses this point.

Despite frequent claims by Communists that there was 'socialist competition' between production units, the near absence of real market forces within Communist economies exerted a negative effect on competition. The attempts to shield Communist economies from the international market compounded the problem of insufficient competition, with all the negative knock-on effects this had on quality, choice, and price.

In theory, their control over the economy meant that Communists were particularly well placed to ensure that economic development was not at the expense of the environment. In practice, the commitment to economic growth at almost any cost typically meant the environment was a low priority, and most East European states had worse environmental problems by the 1980s

10. A large-scale chemical enterprise in East Germany

than their West European counterparts, despite being on average less industrially developed. With the benefit of hindsight, we can see its poor environmental legacy as one of the worst failings of Communist central planning.

A final point about CPEs is that some commentators reject the very use of the term 'centrally planned economies', preferring to refer to 'command economies'. This preference is based on the argument that production priorities were essentially dictated from above, and were based more on political considerations than on the needs of the economy and the population. Use of this term implies that management of the economy was in practice less rational and more subject to arbitrary political control than the term 'planned' suggests.

Attempts at economic reform

By the 1960s, many Communist leaderships were recognizing the need to address problems in their economies, and that if their countries were ever to catch up with and overtake the West, as they were supposed to, changes would have to be made. Thus was introduced a series of economic reform packages that were intended to improve economic performance and the supply of consumer goods. The first of these, the New Economic System, was introduced in East Germany in 1963. The Soviets and Yugoslavs brought in their own version of reform in September 1965 – while what many analysts consider to have been the most radical package was Hungary's New Economic Mechanism, introduced in 1968. While each country's reform package was unique, a number of features were common. One was that economic decision-making was to be partly devolved; the central agencies were to transfer some of their powers to the enterprises. Although Hungary's New Economic Mechanism, which largely did away with central planning, was widely considered to have been the most successful, even its economy had slowed right down by the second half of the 1970s.

Since most of the economic reforms of the 1960s had failed to deliver the desired improvements, many Communist governments introduced further reforms in the 1970s. The most significant in several East European states and the USSR was the amalgamation of several enterprises into one larger unit, usually called an association or combine or corporation, depending on the actual arrangement. These were not entirely new in the 1970s; but there was in several countries a new focus on them and their numbers were significantly increased. Unfortunately for both the Communists and the consumers, economic growth figures reveal that these reforms did not work either.

The performance of CPEs

There are numerous problems involved in attempting to assess the performance of Communist economies. One is that comparison with both non-Communist systems and sometimes even between Communist systems is difficult because of the use of different measurement methods. Thus Yugoslavia used a different method for measuring the overall growth of its economy (Gross Material Product) from that used by China until 1985 and Comecon member states (Net Material Product, NMP), which in turn differed from the method most commonly used for measuring Western economic growth (Gross Domestic Product, GDP). It is not necessary to understand the differences between these methods, but rather the fact that they exist and make direct comparison problematic, and that using NMP instead of GDP makes growth look higher, since it excludes much service activity. At least as serious a problem as the method used is the reliability of the statistics. A number of officials from Communist statistics offices admitted in the 1990s that they had sometimes been required to massage figures for political reasons, so that they would appear more impressive. Sometimes, particularly in the early years, important economic statistics simply were not published by the Communist authorities. Partly because of this, and partly in order to understand better what was happening in the Communist world, both scholars and intelligence agencies in the West used to produce their own estimates. Given all this, economic growth figures for Communist states have to be treated with extreme caution, and should never be fetishized or treated as necessarily being accurate. With these caveats in mind, Table 2 provides an overview of economic growth patterns in several Communist states. Since the basis of these statistics is Communist sources themselves, the most striking point is that most Communist states enjoyed very impressive growth in the 1950s and 1960s, which slowed down in the 1970s, and even more so in the 1980s; Cuba – in the first half of the decade – and China were notable exceptions to the 1980's trend.

Table 2. Average annual economic growth rate (*mostly* net material product produced, in percent) per quinquennium, 1951–89, selected Communist states

	51–5	56–60	61–5	66–70	71–5	76–80	81–5	86–9	86–90 (Plan)
Albania			5.7	8.8			2.0	3.3	c. 6.0
Bulgaria	12.2	9.7	6.7	8.6	7.9	6.1	3.7	3.1	5.4
China	10.9	5.1	5.2	8.0	5.3	5.9	9.3	8.9	7.5
Cuba			3.8	0.4	14.7	3.8	7.3	0.0	5.0
Czecho-slovakia	8.2	7.0	1.9	6.8	5.7	3.7	1.8	2.1	3.4
GDR	13.1	7.1	3.5	5.2	5.4	4.1	4.5	3.1	4.6
Hungary	5.7	5.9	4.7	6.8	6.2	2.8	1.4	0.8	3.0[*]
Poland	8.6	6.6	6.2	6.0	9.7	1.2	−0.8	2.9	3.3[*]
Romania	14.1	6.6	9.1	7.7	11.2	7.2	4.4	1.6	10.3
USSR	11.4	9.2	6.5	7.6	5.7	4.3	3.2	2.7	4.2
Yugoslavia	7.5	11.8	6.5	4.7	5.9	5.6	0.7	0.4	4.0

Note: * Averaged out, between the earlier and later plan estimates.

But overall economic growth is not the only way in which performance can be measured. Given their own stated priorities, the Communist states can also be judged in terms of unemployment rates, inflation, labour productivity, and Gini indices.

Most Communist states claimed to have no structural unemployment. By this they meant that people whose work was no longer required – perhaps because of modernization of techniques in their workplace, for instance – would not be unemployed for an indefinite period because of this. Rather, the person would be retrained, during which time they would be paid. What Communist governments rarely admitted was that there was often *underemployment*, particularly in the countryside. And the most transparent of the Communist systems in Eastern Europe, Yugoslavia, did not attempt to hide unemployment anyway; the official rate was 7.7% in 1970, and 11.9% by 1980 (ILO figures). The unemployment figures for other Communist countries are mostly Western estimates (e.g. 5.4% for Cuba in 1979), although China has in recent years openly acknowledged structural unemployment.

Communist states also often claimed to have little or no inflation. But this claim was disingenuous. Sometimes, the inflation was highly visible, as with the price rises on food that resulted in mass protests in the USSR in 1962 and in Poland on numerous occasions. More frequently, the inflation was hidden, or what economists call repressed. The most obvious sign of this was shortages and rationing; these are signs of imbalance – disequilibrium – in an economy just as much as overt price inflation. By the 1980s, there were long lists of rationed basic foodstuffs in Cuba and Romania, for example; while the lists were shorter in countries such as Poland, their very existence revealed repressed inflation.

In the early years, most Communist economies grew impressively on the basis of extensive methods, notably mobilizing the workforce (i.e. increasing the percentage of people going out to work, typically through mobilization of women). But once an economy has soaked up this additional workforce, further growth requires a more intensive approach. A prime factor in this is to increase labour productivity, making workers more efficient. The problems of innovation and incentive already outlined meant that labour productivity did not increase in most Communist states to anything like the levels necessary if these states were to catch up with and overtake their capitalist rivals.

Although Communist states never claimed to be committed to economic equality, they *were* in theory committed to lower income differentials than in market economies. A common method for measuring income inequality is via Gini coefficients, which are calculated by taking half the expected difference in income between two randomly selected individuals as a proportion of the mean income of a population. In fact, over time analysis of income distribution in the USSR reveals that some periods had much flatter distribution periods than at others, so that policies on this were not consistent. However, a comparison of the Gini coefficients of a number of Communist states in the late 1980s indicates that the gap between rich and poor was narrower than in most Western states. Gini coefficients are often presented on a 0 to 100 (percentage) scale, and are then called the Gini index: the higher the percentage, the wider the income gap, and hence the greater the inequality. In 1986, Czechoslovakia had a Gini index of 19.7% – making it the most egalitarian of the East European countries – compared with 22.1% in Hungary, 24.2% in Poland, and 27.6% in Russia. By way of comparison, the UK index at that time was 26.7% – higher than the East European states just listed, but slightly lower than the Russian figure.

Communist economies generally operated in very different ways from how capitalist economies operate. The state was much more involved in them, and the so-called 'invisible hand' of the market was not merely invisible, but largely non-existent. For all their shortcomings, Communist systems were reasonably effective at transforming largely rural agricultural economies into urban industrial ones. In the early years of Communist power, they were also able to boast high growth rates. However, *most* economies enjoy high growth rates when in transition from a predominantly agricultural to a predominantly industrial base. Moreover, many of the Communist economies had high growth rates in the years following World War II; again, most types of economic system have high growth rates when recovering from a war. Thus, while it is often argued that Communism was an efficient and effective method of modernizing an economy, it must be borne in mind that many non-Communist states performed as well as or better than their Communist counterparts. For example, while China's annual average growth rate 1965–80 initially looks impressive at 6.4%, it was in fact lower than the annual average rates in Brazil, Indonesia, South Korea, and Thailand.

Thus, if we are to focus on the achievements of Communist economies, it would be more on the provision of basic needs – housing, healthcare, education, public transport – for most citizens. Conversely, citizens as consumers of goods were in general poorly served.

But what of the Communist states that have been described in this book as economically post-communist? Under Deng, the Chinese Communists argued that marketization is not incompatible with socialism. This was not a particularly controversial or novel claim, since other Communist states had earlier argued that *elements* of marketization, notably competition between enterprises, were acceptable in a Communist economy. Once marketization had been introduced in China, the next question was whether or not privatization was acceptable. For several years, the Chinese Communists adopted an innovative approach to this; the state continued to own the means of industrial production, but was willing to rent them out to entrepreneurs. But at the end of the 1990s, the Chinese finally passed a law that permitted private ownership of large-scale means of industrial production, such as factories. Did this represent a renunciation of Marxism?

No straightforward answer can be given to this question. One reason is that Marx's views towards the end of his life were in some important areas different from those in his earlier years. But if it is accepted that Marx was generally more inclined towards determinism than voluntarism, then his argument that countries have to proceed through various stages of economic development and be predominantly industrialized and urbanized before they can be ready for socialism and communism means that the Chinese position can be defended. The growth and development of the Chinese economy since the late 1970s has not only been impressive, but has also allowed it to make substantial progress towards catching up with the West. According to the World Bank, China's average annual growth rate between 1987 and 1997 was 10.3%, while it was 9.5% between 1997 and 2007. By the latter date, it had the world's fourth largest economy, according to both the IMF and the World Bank. From the perspective of the Chinese Communists, however, the problem with acknowledging the later Marxist argument on the need to proceed through development stages is that Marx also saw the historical need for a bourgeois democracy preceding a genuinely socialist transformation; while the Chinese Communists have sought *partly* to address this by encouraging wealthy entrepreneurs to join the Communist party, there are unquestionably serious tensions in such an approach. A similar problem will face the Vietnamese Communists. According to the World Bank, Vietnam's annual average growth rate 1987–97 was 7.7%, and 1997–2007 was 7.2% – impressive by almost any criteria. But whether this will be sufficient to protect the Vietnamese Communists against challengers wanting democracy remains to be seen, especially if the economy encounters major problems.

Chapter 5
Social policies and structures of communism

People who have never lived under Communism often find it difficult to understand why there remains nostalgia for the Communist period among elements of the population in many countries. After all, the political system was in practice elitist and basically undemocratic, most consumer goods were in short supply and often of poor quality, and there had been a terror regime in many countries during at least part of the Communist era. In order to understand this nostalgia, it is necessary to explore some of the more positive aspects of Communist power, in particular its social welfare policies. But an understanding of Communist societies also requires consideration of some of the social cleavages in particular countries, and how Communists attempted to deal with these.

Social welfare policies

The provision of collective goods by Communist systems – such as free education, free healthcare, heavily subsidized accommodation (Soviet citizens paid an average of only 3–5% of their income on accommodation at the end of the 1970s, while most Hungarians paid no more than 10%) and public transport, and so on – was so extensive that they have been described as the ultimate 'cradle to grave', 'womb to tomb', or even 'sperm to worm' welfare states.

It was not a Communist country, but rather Wilhelmine Germany, that first introduced the welfare state. The rationale behind this was that a good state should accept responsibility not only to defend its citizens against aggressors, but also to care for them on an ongoing basis. Thus, in 1883 under Chancellor Bismarck, Germany became the first country in the world to establish a compulsory state-run health insurance scheme. A number of other European countries, including Hungary, had well-developed pension, healthcare, and other welfare programmes long before the Communists came to power. Nevertheless, the Communists took the concept of state-provided welfare to new levels. The focus here will be on three elements of this – healthcare, education, and employment.

One of the first social welfare priorities of Communist states was to provide free and universal healthcare. This objective was achieved in the 1920s in the USSR and by the end of the 1940s throughout Communist Eastern Europe. China had near-universal access to the healthcare system by the 1950s, although the system was based on the commune rather than organized by the central state authorities. In line with the country's traditions, the Chinese system was also based more on prevention than on treatment; the East European and Soviet systems were oriented more towards treatment. In short, while Communist systems basically agreed on the need for state provision of healthcare, their approaches on how best to organize this differed; this was partly because of diverse cultural traditions.

One potential indicator of the efficacy of healthcare systems is to consider life expectancy. According to the official statistics, this increased over time in the Communist states. But this is true of most countries – and in any case, it is ultimately not possible to determine the extent to which this is a function of the healthcare system, as distinct from other factors, such as changing dietary or work patterns.

Table 3. Average life expectancy in selected Communist and Western states

	1935	1950	1960	1970	1980	1988	2008
Bulgaria	50.1	<64.1	69.6	71.1	71.1	71.2	n.a.
China		40.8	46.1	61.1	65.4	69.5	73.2
Cuba		59.4	63.8	70	73.1	74.2	77.3
Germany (East)		65.9	68.9	70.7	71.6	72.9	n.a.
Hungary		<63.6	67.8	69	69.2	70.1	n.a.
Poland		<61.3	67.1	70.2	70.9	71.5	n.a.
USSR	46.0		68.6	69.3	67.7	69.5	n.a.
Vietnam	34.0		42.9	47.8	55.8	62.7	71.3
Yugoslavia		58.1		68.0	70.4	71.5	n.a.
Germany (West)	61.3	67.5	69.1	70.8	72.5	75.5	79.1*
Japan	45.0	60.0	66.8	71.1	75.5	79	82.1
UK		68.7	70.4	71.4	72.8	75	78.9
USA		68.2	69.7	70.4	73.3	75.5	78.1

Notes:

1. Most statistics are from the UN database; some are presented only as an average over five years, so that, in these cases, the mean average over a ten-year period has been calculated. Thus most 1950 figures are the mean average of the two figures 1945–50 and 1950–5, rounded up to the nearest decimal point if the average in the second quinquennium was higher than in the first, and rounded down if the later quinquennium had a lower average than the earlier one. Where only one five-year average has been given *starting* from the year cited in a column of the above table, this is indicated by use of a 'less than' sign. Most of the other statistics are directly cited from or calculated on the basis of data in National Statistical Yearbooks.

2. n.a. means not applicable (state is no longer Communist).

* Unified Germany.

Given that life expectancy may not be an accurate reflection of the quality of healthcare in a given country, many analysts prefer to cite infant mortality rates; the lower these are, it is assumed, the more effective the healthcare facilities. Table 4 provides selected data on this; it reveals that most Communist states made

Table 4. Infant mortality rates per 1,000 births in selected Communist and Western states

	1950	1960	1970	1980	1989	2008
Bulgaria	94.5	45.1	27.3	20.2	14.4	n.a.
China	195.0	150.0	85.0	49.0	38.0	23.0
Cuba	32.0	35.9	38.7	19.6	11.1	5.1
Germany (East)	72.2	38.8	18.5	12.1	7.6	n.a.
Hungary	85.6	47.6	35.9	23.2	14.8	n.a.
Poland	111.2	54.8	33.4	21.3	16.0	n.a.
USSR	80.7	35.3	24.7	27.3	25.0	n.a.
Vietnam		70.0	55.0	44.0	38.0	19.5
Yugoslavia	118.6	87.7	55.2	35.0	20.2	n.a.
Germany (West)		34.0	23.4	12.7	7.0	4.3*
Japan	50.6	31.0	14.0	8.0	5.0	3.2
UK	32.0	23.0	18.0	12.0	9.0	4.8
USA	29.2	26.0	20.0	12.6	9.8	6.3

Notes:
1. Figures are for the nearest year to that cited, but are in no case more than two years out.
2. n.a. means not applicable (state is no longer Communist).
* Unified Germany.

impressive progress on this front, with East Germany having a better record by the late 1980s than many Western states. On the other hand, the Soviet Union actually went backwards in the 1970s, and was no better by the end of the 1980s than it had been two decades earlier; the Cuban situation also deteriorated in the first decade of Communist power, but has since made great progress.

One of the many signs in recent years that China was moving away from what most people would expect of a Communist system was the shift away from state provision of healthcare and towards private provision that began in the 1980s. This occurred as its market-oriented economic reforms proceeded, so that by 2002 individual citizens – in most cases, courtesy of their employer – were responsible for approximately two-thirds of overall health expenditure; by the middle of this decade, almost 75% of Chinese citizens were ineligible for state support if they needed medical care. At the beginning of this decade, the World Health Organization evaluated the Chinese healthcare system as one of the world's least fair and proportionately most underfunded. But the Chinese government, realizing that dissatisfaction with the system was growing in many parts of the country, began to introduce a healthcare reform in 2003 designed to assist the rural poor in particular. Another significant reform was announced in 2007. In terms of state assistance in healthcare, then, China has recently been moving back towards what is usually expected of a Communist state. The country aims to have universal access to primary healthcare by 2010. But there has been improvement in Chinese citizens' health anyway, largely because of overall improvements in socioeconomic conditions. Thus life expectancy in 1982 was 68.0 years, and by 2007 had improved to 73.2 years.

The healthcare achievements of most Communist states were significant, and should not be undervalued. On the other hand, nor should they be exaggerated, since there were aspects of healthcare that were less impressive. Sometimes, periods of political extremism even within the Communist system impacted negatively on the healthcare system; this was true of China during both the Great Leap Forward and the Cultural Revolution. Healthcare systems in many Communist countries were highly corrupt, with patients knowing they needed to offer bribes if they were to receive high-quality and timely treatment. In a sense, this was an unofficial form of healthcare privatization. Contrary to what might be expected, most systems were also very hierarchical, with much better facilities available to members of the elite than to ordinary citizens; these were the so-called closed facilities. Many

Communist states used to boast that they had a higher proportion of doctors per head of population than most Western states. But this can indicate either over-servicing or that medical technology is less advanced, necessitating more human input. One clear sign that the healthcare services were not as impressive as they might have been is that life expectancy in some Communist states actually *declined* in more recent decades, after the initial improvements. The best example was the USSR, where life expectancy by 1985 was two years less (at 68.4 years) than it had been in 1964 (70.4 years). But even in those countries in which it did not decline, it did sometimes essentially stagnate in the last two decades of Communist rule, as revealed in Table 3.

Education was another high priority for Communist states. This was in most cases free and compulsory, and the average minimum number of years of schooling rose in most states over time (e.g. from seven to ten years in most parts of the USSR between 1957 and 1970). In terms of improving literacy rates, too, the achievements were impressive, as revealed in Table 5.

While many *non*-Communist states also achieved much in terms of raising literacy rates in the 20th century, the average and pace was often less than that in the Communist world. However, various limitations of the Communist educational systems should be noted. One was that the emphasis was generally on rote-learning, not the development of critical and creative skills; this might be appropriate and effective in some subjects (e.g. learning foreign languages), but it meant that there was very little encouragement by the state of individual initiative. Related to this was the fact that raising literacy rates and the structure of education systems generally were overtly geared towards indoctrinating students with Communist values, in a way that many people with non-Communist backgrounds would find intrusive; this, too, discouraged the development of individual critical thought that many consider a basic right not only in a true democracy but also in

Table 5. Literacy rates in selected Communist and Western states (age 15 +).

	1940	1950	1960	1970	1980	1988	2008
Bulgaria		>75.8		92.4	95.1	98	n.a.
China		>45.0	40	52.9	67.1	>75	90.9
Cuba		<77.9		89.3	92.5	98.5	99.8
Germany (East)		>98.0			99.0	99.0	n.a.
Hungary		95.3		98.1	98.6	99.1	n.a.
Poland		>90.0		98.2	99.1	99.6	n.a.
USSR	87.4	>90.0	98.5	99.7	99.8	99+	n.a.
Vietnam		>20.0			87.3	90.3	93.0
Yugoslavia	55	74.0	80.0	83.5	90.5	93.0	n.a.
Germany (West)		>98.0				99.0	99.0*
Japan		97.8				99.0	99.0
UK		>98.0				99.0	99.0
USA		97.5	98	99.0		99.0	99.0

Notes:
1. Where no figures are available for the actual year cited, those for the nearest year available – never more than three years different – have been included.
2. n.a. means not applicable (state is no longer Communist).
* Unified Germany.

a more egalitarian society. Finally, some of the remaining Communist states have pursued decidedly *un*communist approaches to education in recent years. Vietnam, for instance, has since the 1990s been encouraging the development of the private education sector, and permitting state educational institutions to charge tuition fees.

Structural unemployment as this is now known almost worldwide was not generally a feature of Communist systems. This helps to

11. An early Soviet literacy poster (the caption reads 'Literacy – the Way to Communism')

explain why Russia, for example, did not have any structural unemployment benefits from 1930 until the beginning of the 1990s – they were considered unnecessary – and only opened its first unemployment office in decades in July 1991. It also helps to explain why people who have suffered unemployment and insecurity under post-communism are sometimes nostalgic for the past. As with the other areas of social welfare considered here, however, there were downsides to this job security. From the perspective of the individual, some of the jobs that ensured full employment were monotonous and unchallenging; this can apply to jobs in non-Communist systems too, however, and many people might prefer boring work to unemployment. But from society's perspective, the commitment to full employment discouraged efficiency, which contributed to the long-term decline of most Communist economies from the 1970s onwards. Another negative aspect of Communists' full employment policies was that citizens were not only guaranteed employment but also *required* to work. If an individual wanted to try their luck making a living as an artist, for instance, and was not an approved artist of the state, they were likely to fall foul of the authorities. And in many cases, especially in the years immediately following graduation from a tertiary-level educational institution, citizens were required to work in locations determined by the state, not of their own choice.

Social structure: classes

A common fallacy about Communism is that Communist states claimed to have eradicated social classes. In fact, no Communists in power ever claimed to have eliminated classes. Rather, they typically claimed after several years in power that they had eradicated *antagonistic* classes. Most Communist states maintained that they had two main classes (peasants, workers), where a class was primarily defined as a large social grouping, the members of which shared a common relationship to the means of production. In addition, Communists identified a third group, which was sometimes rendered as white-collar workers or employees, and sometimes as the intelligentsia. This group occupied an intermediate position between classes and was called a 'stratum'. The intelligentsia in Communist systems comprised a much broader group than what most Anglophone people understand by the term. While the stratum did include intellectuals – creative, scientific, critical – the term 'intelligentsia' usually applied to anyone with a completed higher education. Indeed, the concept was often understood broadly enough to include almost all white-collar workers; in other cases, the broad concept of white-collar workers would be subdivided into the higher-ranking and better-educated intelligentsia and lower-level office workers lacking higher education. The Communist position was that none of the three groups – the two main classes and the stratum – *exploited* either of the others, which explains how there could be *non-antagonistic* classes. On the other hand, Communist authorities and sociologists did usually distinguish between mental and manual labour, as well as between the rural and urban workforce. Confusingly, however, people who worked on state farms in the countryside were classified in many countries as workers, while peasants were typically only those who worked on collective farms. From the Communists' perspective, one advantage of this approach to classification is that it made the working class look bigger, thus justifying claims that societies were sufficiently developed in Marxist terms to be socialist. It is doubtful that Marx would have accepted such claims.

These official descriptions of the class structure did not go unchallenged, however. Arguably the greatest critic was not a Western anti-Communist, but someone who had until 1954 been one of the most senior leaders of the Yugoslav Communists, Milovan Djilas. His early criticisms resulted in a long prison sentence, and his best-known and most detailed critique, *The New Class* (first published in the West, in 1957), was written while he was in prison. Djilas maintained that Marxism needed updating to acknowledge changes that had occurred in the 20th century. According to him, Marx's argument that *ownership* of the means of production was the basis of class rule and class oppression was based on the fact that, when Marx was writing in the 19th century, those who owned factories typically also managed them. But by the 20th century, ownership and management had in many cases become separated, as firms expanded and became public companies; ownership typically became more diffuse as large numbers of people purchased shares in them, while managers were often not owners in a formal sense. Yet in 20th-century capitalism, it was increasingly the managers, not the shareholders, who took the most important decisions about production and the conditions of the workforce. Djilas believed that such an argument could be applied to Communist systems. For him, it was the state planners and others, such as the party elite, who took decisions about production and labour. They therefore constituted a new exploitative – and hence antagonistic – class in Communist systems, even if they did not *formally* own the means of production.

Other social cleavages

Classes, whether antagonistic or not, were not the only social cleavages in Communist societies. Two other significant ones were ethnicity and gender.

Like most countries, Communist states were multi-ethnic, though the balance between the largest group and the others varied significantly. Thus, whereas Poland comprised around 98% Poles in the 1980s and Albania 96% Albanians (though these can be subdivided into Ghegs and Tosks), only a little over half of the Soviet population was ethnically Russian, while Serbs comprised less than 40% of the Yugoslav population. Even in most countries with a numerically very dominant ethnic majority, there were sizeable minorities, which often expressed dissatisfaction with their treatment by what they perceived to be a political system essentially controlled by the main ethnic group. For instance, China in the 1980s was 93% Han Chinese, but could not hide the fact that Tibetans in Tibet and Muslim Uighurs in Xinjiang often claimed they were being treated unfairly by the authorities. By the 1980s, there were also clearly tensions between the Romanian authorities and the Hungarian minority, the Hungarian authorities and the Slovak minority, the Bulgarian authorities and the Turkish minority, and several East European states and the Roma. A complete list of ethnic tensions in the Communist world would be much longer.

Some Communist leaderships, such as first Laotian Communist leader Kaysone Phomvihane, argued that it was unrevolutionary and uncommunist to classify people according to their ethnicity; his approach amounted to a refusal to acknowledge ethnic difference and the right of people to claim that. Other leaderships, including the Soviet, did recognize ethnic differences in society, but by the 1970s were claiming optimistically and unrealistically that all fundamental tensions between these groups had been resolved, and that ethnic groups would first merge and then fuse. This approach was derived mainly from Lenin, who, like Marx, believed that national identities and nationalism would gradually disappear as socialism emerged and then progressed into communism. Unfortunately for these leaderships, ethnic conflict did manifest itself overtly from time to time in several Communist states. In the USSR, a prime example was Lithuanian nationalism.

Lithuania's forcible incorporation into the USSR in 1940 helps to explain why so many of its citizens had never really accepted rule from Moscow. In the late 1960s, several Lithuanian Catholic priests began to demand greater religious freedom for their country, which was – and remains – overwhelmingly Catholic. This eventually resulted in the arrest of two priests in 1971, which triggered mass demonstrations. The hostility toward Moscow peaked in 1972. A young man, Romas Kalanta, committed suicide by self-immolation as a way of protesting against Soviet domination. His burial in Lithuania's second city, Kaunas, led to a further mass demonstration, involving thousands of Lithuanians. Although this and other demonstrations were forcibly suppressed by the Soviet authorities, the protests were not completely quelled. But in November 1973, the KGB launched a concerted effort to stop the lingering unrest, and arrested a number of Lithuanian dissidents. Prison sentences of up to six years were imposed on those nationalist dissidents identified as the ringleaders, and this effectively stopped the overt manifestations of Lithuanian anti-Sovietism for many years.

At about the same time as Moscow was dealing with Lithuanian nationalism, Belgrade was trying to placate Croatian nationalists. However, unlike the Lithuanian case, and while Croatia is also a predominantly Catholic country, the nationalism in this case was not directly involved with the Church. Moreover, it was largely elite-led, rather than a popular phenomenon, although the leaders then encouraged mass rallies to support their criticisms of the federal authorities. This period of political unrest is often called the Croatian Spring, since some of its leaders claimed they had been inspired by the Prague Spring of 1968. A number of Croatian leaders were indignant at what they perceived to be unfair treatment by the Yugoslav authorities, and demanded greater autonomy within the federation. A key issue related to economic interests. Croatia was the second wealthiest republic in the Yugoslav federation to no small extent because of the large number of West European tourists it attracted to its beautiful coastline, and several of its senior leaders resented having to exchange most of its foreign currency for the Yugoslav currency at what they considered to be highly unfavourable exchange rates. The head of the Croatian Communists was dismissed in December 1971 for making critical comments on this issue. But this only encouraged party leaders in some of the other republics to vent their open criticisms of the federal leadership, such that Yugoslav leader Tito talked for the first time publicly of a 'national crisis' threatening the country's very existence. This eventually led to a recentralization of power in Yugoslavia in 1974. But the problems had really only been swept under the carpet, not solved.

The clearest sign that many Communist systems had never resolved the issue of ethnic conflict and nationalism, whatever Communist leaderships claimed, was that the three federal Communist states all disintegrated, essentially along ethnic lines, in the 1990s. The USSR was dissolved in December 1991, and Czechoslovakia in December 1992; former Yugoslavia has experienced a protracted and very painful disintegration since this began in 1991, a process that was still underway in 2008.

As with most aspects of Communism in power, the situation regarding gender – particularly the position of women – was mixed; it can be analysed from political, workforce, and domestic situation perspectives.

In theory, Communist governments were highly committed to gender equality, and there were some signs of this commitment in practice. Regarding political representation, there were what initially look like some impressive achievements in the Communist world. For example, Communist states had among the world's highest percentages of women in the legislature, as revealed in Table 6.

But the high percentages of female representation in Communist systems were achieved through having quota systems – unlike the situation in most Western systems, where seats are allocated on the basis of competitive elections. Moreover, it is important to bear in mind that, unlike their Western counterparts, Communist legislatures were generally neither fora for discussion nor independent decision-making bodies; they typically passed laws as directed by other political bodies, such as the Council of Ministers and, in particular, the senior party organs. Given this, it is telling that Communist Politburos – the ultimate decision-making bodies in Communist systems – were overwhelmingly male-dominated. In 1986, the Soviet Politburo had *no* female members; in fact, it had only ever had one female member until the late 1980s (Ekaterina Furtseva, 1956–61), when two new female members were added – one in 1988, the other in 1990. Only one of the 107 members of the Soviet Council of Ministers as of December 1988 – more than 70 years after the October Revolution – was a woman. Moreover, Yugoslavia was the only Communist state ever to have a female

Table 6. Percentage of women in selected Communist and Western legislatures (lower house if bicameral)

	1950	1970	1988	2008
Bulgaria	15.1	17.1	21.0	n.a.
China		17.8	21.3	21.3
Cuba		22.2*	33.9	43.2
Germany (East)	27.5	30.6	32.2	n.a.
Poland	0.0	13.5	20.2	n.a.
USSR	19.6	30.2	31.1	n.a.
Vietnam	2.5	18.2	17.7	25.8
Yugoslavia	3.2	5.8	18.2	n.a.
Australia	0.8	0.0	6.1	26.7
France	7.0	2.1	6.9	18.2
Germany (West)	6.8	6.6	15.4	31.6**
Sweden	9.6	14.0	38.4	47.0
UK	3.3	4.1	6.3	19.5
USA	2.1	2.3	6.7	16.8

Notes:

1. The figure for any given year is based on the figure for the immediately preceding election in that country.

2. n.a. means not applicable (state is no longer Communist).

3. Blank cells indicate either no information or that there had been no parliamentary election.

* 1976 (no earlier appropriate legislature).

** This refers to unified Germany.

prime minister (Milka Planinc); while a similar point can be made about Western states, which have also been very slow to introduce gender equality at the top of the political system, the much more directive nature of Communist states and their putative commitment to greater equality means that it is legitimate to criticize them on this score.

12. **Yugoslav Prime Minister (1982–6) Milka Planinc**

Another way in which the level of gender equality can be assessed is to consider it in the workforce. Here, two variables – income and the division of labour – will be examined. In terms of income, Communist states generally performed no better and no worse than their Western counterparts. By the late 1980s, for instance, women earned on average only 66–75% (depending on the country) of what men working in the same profession earned. This was in part because women tended to occupy lower positions in any given profession's hierarchy. The division of labour in Communist states was also rather similar to that in the West, in that women were heavily over-represented in some professions – notably the so-called caring professions such as healthcare and teaching – and under-represented in others. But even in the more feminized professions, the percentage of men increased markedly further up the hierarchy.

Domestically, too, women were often subject to the same extra workloads in Communist countries as they have been in most types of society. Often, they were under pressure to go out to work to earn a living, but then had to perform most or all of the household chores when they returned home. This double burden would become a triple burden if they also had to bear and look after children. While some Communist states helped families with this third task, others were much less accommodating. For example, whereas East Germany offered some of the best childcare facilities in the world – free or very inexpensive, and readily available in most parts of the country – facilities were scarce in many parts of Poland.

Communist states interfered in women's private lives in very different ways and to varying degrees. For instance, the authorities in different countries adopted radically different policies towards childbirth and abortion. The USSR strongly encouraged childbirth – even awarding 'Mother Heroine of the Soviet Union' status to women who bore and raised ten or more children! – yet also made access to abortion relatively easy. China from 1979 forbade women from having more than one child; although this meant that access to abortion was liberal, the state also sometimes forcibly sterilized women who fell pregnant a second time. Romania under Ceauşescu (in power 1965–89) encouraged childbearing to such an extent that childless couples and single women who had not borne children by age 25 years were financially penalized unless they could provide medical evidence of an inability to conceive. Unsurprisingly, given the government's priority of increasing birth rates, abortions became increasingly difficult to obtain in Ceauşescu's Romania.

It can be seen that in the social sphere, as in others, the Communist record is mixed; it varied, sometimes considerably, according to time and country. And some of the remaining Communist states have moved away from Communist policies in recent years, but are now revisiting their decisions.

Chapter 6
Communism's international allegiances

A fundamental tenet of Marxism is that socialism has to be an international movement. It is therefore not surprising that many Communist states sought closer ties with each other. While many Communist leaders claimed that this was primarily for principled reasons of socialist internationalism, there were also solid practical grounds for closer collaboration. Above all, cooperation could have economic and security-related advantages. However, it will be shown that there were also major international tensions in the Communist world – including one that looked as if it could develop into a major war.

Ideological blocs: Comintern and Cominform

Given their different cultures and levels of economic development, as well as the ambiguities and contradictions in the classics of communist theory, it is not surprising that Communist states sometimes interpreted both the theory and the world around them in different ways. Much of the time, and despite Soviet claims of ideological unity, Communist states tacitly agreed to differ over their interpretations. This was particularly true from the 1950s onwards, and helps to explain why the last of the attempts at creating a reasonably homogeneous ideological bloc was abandoned in 1956.

The first attempt by the Soviet Union to establish an international umbrella organization that could unite like-minded parties from around the world resulted in the creation of the Comintern (Communist International, sometimes called the Third International) in 1919. This initially comprised both Communist parties and some of the more radical socialist parties, but soon became more exclusive. In its earliest years, one of the tasks of the Comintern was to export revolution and support attempts at overthrowing 'bourgeois' governments. But from the mid-1920s, the organization was increasingly geared towards supporting and justifying Stalin's statements and actions, as Lenin's successor sought to build Socialism in One Country. But Comintern also dictated how Communist parties were to react to other left-wing parties – and its message was inconsistent. In the early 1930s, Communist parties were instructed not to collaborate with moderate left-wing parties; indeed, they were to undermine them. But this policy changed dramatically in 1935, when Communist parties were expected to cooperate with other left-wing parties in Popular Fronts, as a way of countering the growing attraction of fascism in France, Spain and elsewhere. The dissolution of the Comintern came in May 1943. Until 1941, the Comintern had portrayed World War II as a war between national bourgeois classes, and urged workers not to participate. But once the USSR had been invaded by Nazi Germany and the Soviets became allies of Western countries fighting Germany, it had to do an about-face. This again undermined Comintern's credibility, and it soon folded.

After the end of World War II, Moscow again wanted to establish an umbrella organization that would give it greater control over the international Communist movement. It therefore established Cominform (the Communist Information Bureau) in Poland in September 1947. Cominform was formally created to coordinate and facilitate information flows between European Communists – not only in Eastern Europe (excluding Albania and what was later to become East Germany), but also including the two most significant Communist parties in Western Europe, the French and Italian – and to create a solid ideological bloc to oppose capitalism and imperialism. In reality, Cominform was first and foremost an agency designed to enhance Soviet domination over other parties. In the early stages, it also had the particular brief of ensuring that Communist states did not accept the post-War recovery assistance being offered to European countries by the USA. But Cominform was not a particularly active body from the late 1940s, and especially following Stalin's death. By 1956, Khrushchev had decided that the history of tensions between Yugoslavia and Cominform rendered the continued existence of the organization incompatible with his recent overtures to Belgrade. Cominform was thus dissolved in April 1956.

A military bloc: the Warsaw Pact

It is often wrongly assumed that the Soviets decided to create a Communist military bloc as a direct response to the establishment of a military bloc in the West, the North Atlantic Treaty Organization (NATO). But NATO was formed in April 1949, whereas what is often seen as its Communist counterpart, the Warsaw Pact (formally the Warsaw Treaty Organization or WTO) was not created until May 1955. While the existence of NATO undoubtedly acted as a longer term stimulus to the establishment of the Warsaw Pact, there were also more immediate factors in the mid-1950s.

The principal reason cited by Moscow itself related to an October 1954 meeting of the Western allies in Paris, at which it was decided to upgrade West Germany's status and integrate it better into the Western alliance. This resulted in the transfer of sovereignty to the Federal Republic, its remilitarization, and its inclusion in both NATO and the Western European Union (WEU) in May 1955. The WEU was a new West European defence organization; its establishment, and the ending of the formal occupation of Germany, was perceived by Moscow as a threat. Given the USSR's experience of German invasion less than fifteen years earlier and the impressive way that the post-war West German economy was developing, this perception was not difficult to understand. The founding members of the Warsaw Pact were Albania, Bulgaria, Czechoslovakia, Hungary, Poland, Romania, and the USSR, while East Germany joined in 1956; Albania formally terminated its membership in 1968, having *de facto* ceased to participate at the beginning of the 1960s.

While Germany's changed status was unquestionably a major factor leading the USSR to propose and create the Warsaw Pact, it was not the only consideration. Another related to possible challenges to Soviet hegemony *within* the Communist bloc. At the same time as Germany's status was changed, the occupation of Austria by the victorious allies, including the USSR, was also ended. One condition of this changed status was that Austria had to agree to be a neutral country. Hungary, next door to Austria and now in the Soviet camp, had been closely tied to Austria between 1867 and 1918 in the Austro-Hungarian Empire, and a number of scholars have argued that the USSR was concerned that Hungary would seek a similar neutral status to Austria's. Had this been allowed, Moscow would have lost its right to station troops in Hungary, and its hold over the country would almost certainly have been loosened. The USSR was not prepared to allow this to happen, as became abundantly clear in 1956.

The argument that the Warsaw Pact existed in fact more to keep its member states under the Soviet thumb than as a counterweight to the West has been put forward by Robin Remington. In support of her thesis, she points out that the only time Warsaw Pact troops actually saw action was in suppressing the Prague Spring in 1968. Her argument is persuasive. On the other hand, it should also be borne in mind that one member of the WTO (other than Czechoslovakia itself!) – Romania – refused to participate in the invasion, and that leaders of most of the East European states had

13. Warsaw Pact invasion of Czechoslovakia (1968)

been at least as keen as the Soviet leadership to suppress what they saw as a potentially contagious development in Czechoslovakia. After all, were the Prague Spring ideas to spread and be adopted, their own positions would be threatened.

As Communism began to collapse in Eastern Europe and the Soviet Union, so the *raison d'être* for the Warsaw Pact disappeared, and it was formally dissolved in July 1991. The new president of Czechoslovakia at that time, Vaclav Havel, subsequently wrote that he saw the dissolution of this military alliance as his greatest achievement; given the invasion of his country by the Warsaw Pact in 1968, his passionate hatred of it is understandable.

An economic bloc: Comecon

While membership of the Soviet-dominated military bloc was restricted to the USSR and East European states, the most significant economic bloc in the Communist world eventually included two Asian member states and the sole Latin American Communist state. The Council for Mutual Economic Assistance (CMEA), better known as Comecon, was founded in Warsaw in January 1949. It thus pre-dated both the European Economic Community (the EEC, subsequently incorporated under a different name into the EU), which was formed in 1957, or even its predecessor, the European Coal and Steel Community (created in 1952 as a result of the 1951 Treaty of Paris). Comecon's initial membership comprised Albania, Bulgaria, Czechoslovakia, Hungary, Poland, Romania, and the USSR; East Germany joined in 1950, Mongolia in 1962, Cuba in 1972, and Vietnam in 1978. As with the Warsaw Pact, Albania *de facto* stopped being involved in the early 1960s, and formally quit Comecon in 1968.

Again as with the Warsaw Pact, Comecon was proposed by the USSR primarily because of its own interests. While the timing of its establishment did not relate to the EEC, it *was* in part a response to the West. In mid-1947, the USA announced the Marshall Aid Program, or Marshall Plan. This was an economic revival project designed to help European states recover after World War II. Moscow's initial response to the plan was positive. But it became increasingly clear that there were strings attached to the aid, and Moscow soon interpreted the plan as an attempt by Washington to exercise more leverage in Europe. While there was unquestionably some truth to this, it should also be acknowledged that part of the reason for the American policy was to place it in a stronger position to stave off any potential resurgence of fascism. Moscow saw the US offer as an attempt either to limit or even to reduce the USSR's influence in newly Communist Eastern Europe. And indeed, Czechoslovakia and Poland had initially indicated their intention to apply for US assistance. Moscow stepped in and forbade these two states from participating in the Marshall Plan, but then felt obliged to offer an alternative. An added stimulus came in April 1948, when the OEEC (Organization for European Economic Cooperation) was set up as a direct result of the Marshall Plan; it involved eighteen European states, and had as its first objective the drawing up and implementation of a European Recovery Programme. Just months later, the Soviets made clear their response: the establishment of an international economic zone comprising Communist states.

The establishment of Comecon did not initially result in anything substantial, and the organization was close to moribund for the first decade. A clear symbol of this was that it did not even have a Statute defining the organization's objectives until December 1959. Comecon did become more active in the early 1960s; but as it did, so it encountered problems. The most significant surfaced in 1962. In June, the USSR had proposed a deeper and clearer division of labour between the Comecon member states. While East Germany and Poland appeared to be enthusiastic about the suggestion that they would concentrate more on industrial manufacturing, some of the more southerly members of the bloc, in particular Romania, resented the Soviet proposal. As they saw it, this would force them to remain relatively underdeveloped agrarian countries. The Romanian Communists pointed out that Marx had argued that socialism and communism require all countries to be highly developed economically, and so were able to charge the Soviets with distorting or ignoring Marx. The Soviets were in a vulnerable position, since there was a danger that Romania, and possibly other countries in Comecon, would simply leave the organization and *de facto* move into the Chinese camp, as Albania had already done. By the middle of 1963, Moscow had essentially shelved its plans for a new division of labour.

Comecon remained a rather ineffectual body until the late 1960s. But by then the Soviet leadership had changed, and the new team was determined not to allow their country to be humiliated as it had been in the early 1960s. Following the Soviet-led Warsaw Pact invasion of Czechoslovakia in 1968, Moscow became far more assertive. Even Romania fell more into line; with the chaos of the Cultural Revolution at its height, the attraction of China as a possible alternative Communist hegemon to the USSR waned. In this context, Comecon became much more active, and in June 1971 adopted a 'Complex Programme' that envisaged higher levels of integration and specialization in the member states. The Programme did result in more coordination and interaction between the member states in the 1970s. However, although Comecon was able to promote a greater division of labour between the member states, this was on a branch basis (e.g. within engineering) rather than a sectoral one (e.g. agriculture versus industry); the Soviets had learnt their lesson from the early 1960s. Nevertheless, new tensions soon emerged. Following the 1973 oil crisis, the USSR proposed that the price of primary resources within Comecon should be related to world market prices, but with a time-lag. As a country rich in natural resources, including oil, this arrangement – which was adopted in 1975 – suited the Soviet Union. But some of its resource-poor East European neighbours resented having the new system essentially imposed on them, especially when world oil prices came down and they were still required to pay the Comecon lagged (and hence higher) prices.

Tensions between Comecon member states continued throughout the 1980s, with many of the smaller East European states believing they would fare better if they had greater freedom to interact with Western markets, and the USSR sometimes criticizing fellow member states for inadequate support in developing its natural resources. Few tears were shed when Comecon was dissolved in June 1991.

Divisions and competition in the communist world

Despite their alleged commitment to socialist internationalism, there were often serious tensions between Communist states. One of the first to emerge was between Yugoslavia and the USSR. The fact that the Yugoslav Communists had come to power without Soviet assistance meant they were less beholden to Moscow than most of the other Communist states. Nevertheless, in its first three or so years under Communist rule, Yugoslavia recognized the USSR as the leader of the world Communist movement. But in 1948, it became clear that relations between Moscow and Belgrade had soured. In some ways, it was surprising that this had happened so quickly; after all, the headquarters of the Soviet-dominated Cominform had been established in Belgrade the previous year, suggesting that Yugoslavia was perceived by Moscow to be a loyal supporter of the USSR. But signs of tension became obvious early in 1948, when Moscow delayed negotiations on a trade treaty with Yugoslavia. Stalin wanted to consolidate his hold on the whole of Communist Eastern Europe, and began to claim that the USSR had played a major role in bringing the Yugoslav Communists to power. This was quite untrue. The relationship between Stalin and Tito rapidly deteriorated, and Stalin orchestrated the shock expulsion of Yugoslavia from the Cominform in June 1948. Initially, Tito attempted to placate the Soviet Communists. But by 1949, it was clear that this attempt had failed, and that Yugoslavia was being treated as a pariah by the rest of the Communist bloc – to such an extent that, by the end of that year, Yugoslavia had begun to accept aid from the West.

Relations between Moscow and Belgrade began to thaw after Stalin's death, and the Soviet and Yugoslav Communists reached a *modus vivendi*. Although Yugoslavia never returned fully into the Soviet fold, neither did it side with the West during the Cold War. Rather, together with a number of developing countries such as India, Indonesia, Egypt, and Ghana, it played a major role in the establishment and running of the Non-Aligned Movement (NAM) that was established in 1955. On Tito's initiative, the first NAM summit was held in Belgrade in 1961. According to the NAM's 1979 Havana Declaration, one of the movement's key objectives was to resist all forms of hegemony and to remain neutral *vis-à-vis* Great

14. A meeting of Non-Aligned Movement leaders in 1956: Yugoslav leader Tito (centre) with Egyptian President Nasser (left) and Indian Prime Minister Nehru (right)

Power and bloc politics. While another Communist member of the NAM, Cuba, in practice often sided with the USSR, Communist Yugoslavia maintained an independent stance for most of the Cold War era.

Yugoslavia was not the only South-East European Communist state to challenge Moscow. Albania, which was the only other East European country in which the Communists had taken power with essentially no Soviet involvement, initially pledged its loyalty to Moscow. But its hardline leader Enver Hoxha was dismayed when Khrushchev denounced Stalin in 1956, calling the Soviet Communists 'revisionists'. By the early 1960s, Tirana had realigned itself, this time with China. But when China itself renounced its hardline approach following Mao's death, Albania turned against Beijing too. By the end of the 1970s, it was isolated within Europe; its only real ally from then on was another small Stalinist state, North Korea.

While Yugoslav and Albanian criticisms of the USSR were embarrassing to Moscow, they did not threaten the 'home of socialism'. But by 1969, the deterioration of relations between Moscow and Beijing – the Sino-Soviet rift – was such that some commentators were speculating on the possibility of a major war. Like the Albanian leadership, the Chinese was uncomfortable with the criticisms new Soviet leader Khrushchev was making of Stalin from 1956 on, although they initially kept much of this concern to themselves. In some ways their unease was ironic, since Stalin had not always supported the Chinese Communists as strongly against their enemy, the Chinese nationalists (*Guomindang*), as might have been expected. But Mao admired Stalin's achievements in developing the USSR, as well as his concept of Socialism in One Country.

There had been signs of tension between the two Communist giants even before 1956, in part because the Soviets believed that China was attempting to build its own empire in Asia and Africa, which they feared could one day challenge Moscow's leadership of the world Communist movement. But Beijing's increasingly open unease about Khrushchev's attacks on his predecessor led to an overt exchange of abuse in the late 1950s, with the Chinese accusing the Soviets of being 'revisionists', and the Soviets calling the Chinese 'dogmatists'. In June 1959, the Soviets broke a promise they had made to supply China with nuclear weapons, which Beijing saw as a major slight, and which encouraged Chinese ideologists to intensify their criticisms of the USSR. This reached a pitch in 1960, when the Chinese published a series of strongly worded articles in which they accused the Soviets of having renounced Leninism. The Soviets responded by abandoning a number of major projects in China, leaving bridges and buildings half-constructed. The Sino-Soviet rift was now very public.

Relations continued to deteriorate throughout the 1960s, and peaked in March 1969 when serious fighting broke out between China and the USSR on the Ussuri River, which formed part of the

Sino-Soviet border. There had been numerous incidents in the area since late 1967, with the Chinese accusing the Soviets of incursions into Chinese territory (the Sino-Soviet border was one of the world's longest, at almost 4,400 km); but their intensity increased significantly in March 1969, when Chinese troops fired on Soviet troops on Damansky (Russian name)/Zhenbao (Chinese) Island, situated on the Ussuri River. This round of fighting was short-lived, lasting just hours; but more than 30 Soviet troops had been killed, along with an unspecified number of Chinese troops. Less than a fortnight later, the Soviets retaliated in the area, losing some 60 troops in the process. Skirmishes, both in the Ussuri River area and elsewhere along the Sino-Soviet frontier, continued until September, at which point both sides made conciliatory gestures; the fighting was over.

The 1969 events can in hindsight be said to have had some positive results. For the rest of the world, the most significant were that two major nuclear powers – the Soviets had tested their first nuclear

15. The Ussuri River conflict 1969

weapon in 1949, while China had tested its first atomic bomb in 1964 – had avoided nuclear warfare, and that China now changed its approach towards the West, fearing that the USSR and the West could gang up on the East Asian giant. Beijing's much less aggressive stance towards the capitalist West was soon noted and rewarded; China was admitted to the UN in 1971 – replacing the Republic of China (Taiwan) – and US President Richard Nixon visited China on a goodwill mission in February 1972. A positive result from the perspectives of Moscow and Beijing was that both sides seem to have appreciated how close they had come to major war, and that this could all too easily have developed into a nuclear one.

But this realization did not result in a sudden warming of relations between the Communist giants, which were cool for much of the 1970s. While this suited the West, especially the USA, it did not reflect well on what was supposed to be the international solidarity of Communism. With a more pragmatic leadership coming to power in Beijing in the late 1970s, however, the chances of an improvement looked promising. Unfortunately, Moscow's support of the Vietnamese invasion of Cambodia at the end of 1978 and its own invasion of Afghanistan in 1979 soon muddied the waters again. China had supported the Khmer Rouge regime that had taken power in Cambodia in 1975, and strongly condemned Vietnam's attempts to overthrow this. Moreover, China shared a border with Afghanistan, and did not appreciate having more Soviet troops stationed so near to its own territory.

But pragmatism eventually led the Chinese to respond positively to Soviet overtures for negotiations. One of the stimuli to this change was the fact that the US now had a much more anti-Communist president, Ronald Reagan. Beijing appears to have decided to balance its relations with the two superpowers, in what can be called equidistancing. In this situation, China and the USSR engaged in a series of negotiations through the 1980s. These focused on several issues of concern to China, including the Soviet presence in Afghanistan and support for Vietnam in Cambodia; Soviet influence in Mongolia, which had in Chinese imperial times been largely under Chinese control; and the Sino-Soviet border. The last of these was perhaps the most important long term, and was also a highly complex issue. Not only was there a need for agreement on the demarcation of the frontier itself, but also on a number of border-related matters. These included disputes over access to natural resources in the border region; concern in both Beijing and Moscow that the other side might seek to incite ethnic unrest among groups straddling the border; and Chinese unease that Soviet nuclear missiles had been stationed so close to the border.

These were difficult issues to resolve to mutual satisfaction, and it is not surprising that only limited progress was made through most of the 1980s. Moreover, China continued to be wary of what it saw as the USSR's proclivity to interfere with other countries' sovereignty. Nevertheless, a symbol of Beijing's somewhat less confrontational position on this was its replacement of the term it had used in the 1960s and 1970s to describe Soviet foreign policy, 'social imperialism', with the slightly less critical 'hegemonism'. With the major changes in Soviet foreign policy at the end of the 1980s, such as the withdrawal from Afghanistan and Moscow's changed position on Vietnam's involvement on Cambodia, the way was open for further improvement. But before much could happen, the USSR collapsed.

In part as a ramification of the Sino-Soviet dispute, China sought to enhance its influence in the developing world from the 1960s onwards. The USSR had at that time been signing Treaties of Friendship with a number of so-called Third World states in the Middle East and Africa (e.g. Angola, Iraq, Libya, and Syria), which in practice gave it influence over the way ruling parties in these countries were structured. Like the Soviet Union, China was keen both to increase its political influence and to secure supplies of natural resources, so that it too began to interact more with the developing world. Since the Soviet and Chinese approaches often involved offers to invest in a given country, many Third World states benefited from competition between the Communist giants. This competition also meant that developing states were even less dependent on Western aid and advice than they would have been had they been able to seek assistance from only one major Communist power.

The Soviet Union was not the only Communist state to be accused of aggression because of the invasion of other Communist states. As noted above, Vietnam invaded Cambodia in late 1978. In many ways, the objective and justification was similar to the USSR's in Afghanistan a year or so later – to replace hardline Communists who were giving Communism a bad name with more moderate Communists. The Khmer Rouge in Cambodia under Pol Pot had been engaging in mass genocide, as captured in the powerful 1984 film *The Killing Fields*. The Vietnamese were able to remove the Khmer Rouge from power and install a new pro-Vietnamese and less extremist Cambodian government under Heng Samrin in January 1979. But the Khmer Rouge was not completely beaten, and sporadic fighting between the two groups of Communists continued for years. In terms of inter-Communist conflict, it is germane to note here that China invaded Vietnam in February 1979 because of a series of what Beijing called 'provocative' acts by Hanoi, including the invasion of Cambodia. But the Chinese found the Vietnamese to be a much tougher enemy than expected, and withdrew within less than a month. Vietnam finally left Cambodia in late 1989.

It is clear that different Communist states sometimes had fundamentally different interpretations of the basic principles of communism, which could result in serious tensions between them. In fact, and in line with many realist approaches to international relations, individual Communist states often placed their own interests ahead of socialist internationalism, and it would not be too cynical to argue that the principal advocate of closer cooperation, the USSR, often had its own selfish reasons for promoting this. It is also clear that socialist internationalism did not mean equality between Communist states. The reality was that larger, more powerful states were in a position to bully smaller ones, and that they sometimes took advantage of this; other countries' sovereignty was no more sacred to some Communist states than it has been to many Western states.

Chapter 7
The collapse of communism – and the future

By the early 1990s, only five of the more than twenty Communist states – or seventeen, if a narrower definition is adopted – that had existed in the late 1980s had survived. Of these, three had changed so much that their claims to being Communist could be challenged. Thus China, Vietnam, and Laos had been introducing such radical market-oriented economic changes that it was increasingly misleading to describe their economies and social structures as Communist, though this applied more to China than to Vietnam or Laos. For different reasons, the fourth state about which serious questions could be raised was North Korea; Marx and Lenin would have turned in their graves at the notion of hereditary leadership – a dynasty – in a so-called Communist system. The North Korean system was also functioning poorly. The remaining country, Cuba, was by most criteria also in a sorry state, with widespread poverty.

How had all this happened? After all, the USSR had at one time been the only state capable of challenging the USA, and one of only two superpowers in the world. Moreover, though never a classic empire as this term is usually understood, the Soviet Empire had been a powerful one. But 1991 witnessed the collapse of the Soviet-dominated Communist economic bloc, the Soviet-dominated Communist military bloc, and then of the USSR itself. This was all the more amazing since the West had foreseen none of this. The sudden collapse of Communism was in many ways *the* most surprising event of the 20th century. A number of theories have been posited as to what caused this collapse; some are very specific, while others are more abstract. Some are more a background variable – setting the scene for collapse – while others are more immediate trigger factors. Most are not mutually exclusive, and can be combined for a richer and deeper interpretation. Since the USSR was the key player in the collapse of Communist power, it will feature strongly in the following analysis.

The Gorbachev factor

For those who want to single out any one person as 'responsible' for the collapse of Communist power in Eastern Europe and the USSR, Gorbachev is the favourite target. His role in the collapse has been explained mainly in terms of his personality and his policies.

Gorbachev had – and has! – a personality that is more inclined towards compromise than confrontation. In this, his personality is quite different from the more assertive nature of many of his predecessors. A tendency to seek the middle ground and attempt to garner as much support from a diverse range of interests as possible is often a desirable trait in a leader. But some have argued that in a crisis situation such as the USSR was in by the late 1980s, this type of personality can imply weakness, which others may then exploit.

When Gorbachev came to power in 1985, he was fully aware of the USSR's severe problems. This was why he introduced first *perestroika* (economic restructuring), then *demokratizatsiya* (limited democratization of the political system) and, in particular, *glasnost'* (openness). But he was ultimately unable to control the criticism and open dissatisfaction that *glasnost'* unleashed. Some citizens took advantage of the new openness and tolerance to begin advocating separatist nationalism. Gorbachev himself sometimes

16. Last Soviet leader Mikhail Gorbachev

recognized a need to limit *glasnost'*, even if this was not nearly as often as some of his conservative comrades in the Politburo would have liked. He also dealt firmly with some of the nationalist movements that arose (e.g. in Azerbaijan in 1990 and in Lithuania in 1991; it should however be noted that the violence of the Soviet authorities in the latter case may not have been sanctioned by Gorbachev). But it was too little, too late; he had lost control.

While *glasnost'* at home – in the USSR – had opened Pandora's Box, aspects of Gorbachev's foreign policy have also been seen to have played a key role in the collapse of Communist power. In foreign policy, Gorbachev sought better relations with the West, in line with his policy of 'new political thinking'. But his belief that part of the reason for his country's economic problems was its support for other countries to the detriment of the Soviet citizenry also had major implications for the collapse of Communism. Given the events in Hungary 1956 and Czechoslovakia in 1968, his Sinatra Doctrine was initially met with caution and even scepticism in other Communist countries. But once Gorbachev had completed the withdrawal of Soviet troops from Afghanistan (January 1989) and urged the Vietnamese leadership to withdraw its troops from neighbouring Cambodia, East Europeans began to believe that they really were free at last to choose their own fate without Soviet interference.

There is no question that Gorbachev's role in the collapse of Communism was critical. But no one person could single-handedly bring about an historic event of such a magnitude; the preconditions, in this case the rottenness and long term decline of Communism, had to exist. Moreover, it is ironic that many of those who criticize Gorbachev most strongly were also harsh critics of Communism. Their position is contradictory, hypocritical even. The world should be grateful to Gorbachev for the significant role he played in the almost peaceful collapse of Communist power and the end of the Cold War. Admittedly, he lost control of both processes towards the end, and he had not intended the first

17. Toppled Lenin statue (Estonia)

of them to go as far as it did. But had it not been for Gorbachev's policies and overall approach, the eventual outcomes would not have occurred when and how they did.

Imperial overstretch

The USSR was sometimes described as an empire. For those subscribing to this view, it comprised an inner and an outer component. The inner empire was the USSR itself – fifteen republics, fourteen of them dominated by Russia. The outer empire comprised putatively sovereign states that owed their allegiance to Russia and were linked to it formally, via the Warsaw Pact and/or Comecon. For some observers, even states that were in neither of these organizations but that were basically in the Soviet camp, such as Angola or Afghanistan, were also part of the Soviet outer empire. To the extent that the USSR, and in particular Russia, was the centre of a vast empire, a theory of the collapse of empires can be applied to it.

In a best-selling book published in 1987, *The Rise and Fall of the Great Powers*, Yale-based British historian Paul Kennedy analysed the collapse of empires down the ages, and argued that a major reason for their failure was 'imperial overstretch'. In a nutshell, Kennedy related the decline of empires to economic decline, which in turn was a function of excessive expenditure on the military.

Unfortunately for him, Kennedy did not apply his own argument to the Soviet Union. Had he done so, he would have been one of the few Western observers to predict the collapse of the USSR – and the 'Soviet Empire'. Nevertheless, his basic argument accords well with Gorbachev's own analysis of the reasons for the problems his country was facing by the mid to late 1980s. The Soviet economy was slowing down, and was heavily skewed towards military expenditure. But – and here we move beyond Gorbachev – the Soviet Empire was a strange one. Most empires exist at least in part to enhance the economic strength of the imperial power. But the Soviet Empire existed more for ideological and political reasons than for economic advantage. Indeed, parts of the empire – even of the inner empire – had a higher standard of living than Russia itself. Despite the unusual nature of the Soviet empire, Kennedy's basic argument fits the collapse well. Although it applies mainly to the USSR, the latter's developing crisis had knock-on effects in other Communist states. Conversely, the fact that China did not seek to create an empire in the way the USSR did helps to explain its continued existence.

Economic failure

The marked slowdown in the growth rates of most Communist states – certainly those in Europe and the USSR – by the 1980s meant that most countries were failing to meet their own plan targets as well as falling behind the West. Since socialism and eventually communism was supposed to be superior to capitalist liberal democracy, this was a severe embarrassment to Communist governments.

But declining growth rates reflected deeper problems with the economies of most Communist states, such as the increasing complexity and overload of central planning; state monopolization; the negative implications of the ratchet principle on innovation; and the inability to redress the imbalance caused by years of privileging heavy industry and defence.

One other factor to include here is that Comecon had attempted to isolate itself from world markets – from what was by the 1990s being called economic globalization – and had failed. While globalization itself has been widely questioned in light of the 2007–8 global economic crisis, its basic ideology was in the ascendancy in the late 1980s, and it can be argued that the USSR's attempts to remain outside of the near-global trend towards freer financial, trade, and to some extent labour markets was unrealistic. Thus the positive effects of globalization largely bypassed the Communist world, whose claims to superiority sounded increasingly hollow. Citizens in Communist states were aware of this, and became ever more dissatisfied with and cynical about their system.

Competition with the West

Ever since Stalin's claims that socialism could be achieved in one country and that this could be a model for other countries to emulate, the USSR and several other Communist states saw themselves as being in competition with the West. It became a major and explicit objective of countries such as the Soviet Union, Bulgaria, East Germany, and China to catch up with and overtake the West.

In addition to economic competition, the USSR was in military competition with the West for much of its existence. But a new chapter in this was opened during the 1980s, when the USA announced its Strategic Defence Initiative (SDI), popularly known as Star Wars. In fact, the American authorities acknowledged in the 1990s that the US had not progressed nearly as far with its development of this technology as the rest of the world believed.

But the Soviet authorities recognized in the 1980s that they could not afford to compete with this new form of defence. In a sense, they were acknowledging that they could not overtake the West. While recent archival material suggests that it is easy to overstate the significance of SDI in the Communists' decision essentially to 'throw in the towel', some senior officials in the Reagan administration highlighted this factor.

The role of dissidents and other opposition forces

The Western media began in the late 1960s to focus on the fate of citizens – particularly critical intellectuals – in Communist states who dared to challenge the authorities. Some of these intellectual dissidents were clearly anti-Communist, such as Solzhenitsyn. Others, such as East German dissident Wolfgang Harich, considered themselves 'true Marxists', for whom the Communists had distorted Marx's ideas and ideals, and had turned Communism into a bureaucratic and hierarchical system. Quite how much influence individual dissidents had on the collapse of Communist power is difficult to determine, and in any case varies from country to country. But even though he was elected by parliament, Czech dissident Vaclav Havel's subsequent popularity as Czechoslovakia's first post-communist president indicates that Czechs and Slovaks were aware of his ideas and were inspired by him to challenge the Communist authorities. In 1978, Havel had clandestinely – through *samizdat*, meaning self-publication – published a powerful extended essay, *The Power of the Powerless*, in which he argued that most citizens in Communist states were alienated victims forced to live a lie. But having criticized his fellow Czechs and Slovaks for passively accepting this role, he also argued that they *could* challenge the Communist states; powerless citizens could empower themselves initially by refusing to live the lie of Communist propaganda.

But it was not only individual dissidents who challenged the authorities and played a role in undermining Communist power.

18. Czech dissident playwright and post-Communist president Vaclav Havel (1989)

The role of Solidarity in Poland was crucial and inspirational. In some countries, notably the GDR and to a lesser extent Poland and Hungary, the Church also played an important role. From the early 1980s, the Lutheran Church in East Germany acted as a focal point for many disenchanted and critical citizens, including atheists. While it played a less direct and significant role in undermining Communism than Solidarity did, sections of the Catholic Church in Poland also acted as a focal point for discontented citizens, especially after former Polish Cardinal Wojtyla became Pope (John Paul II) in 1978.

Religion and nationalism are often linked, and nationalists were another challenge to the Communists. This was clearly so in the USSR, where nationalists wanting independence – particularly in the Baltic States and Georgia – took advantage of *glasnost'* to push their claims. Another example is Romania, where Hungarian protestors living mainly in Transylvania played a key role in triggering nation-wide protests against the Ceauşescu regime; their initial demonstrations were led by a priest, Father Tokes.

The Marxist corrective

An interesting theoretical approach to the collapse of Communism can be called the Marxist corrective. According to this argument, the voluntarist Marxists had artificially forced the pace of history during the 20th century, and this had eventually rebounded on them. The fact that the international socialist revolution Lenin had expected towards the end of World War I did not materialize meant that Stalin could justify his policy of attempting to build socialism in a country clearly not ready for this by classical Marxist criteria. An important question raised by this approach is whether or not Marx will prove correct in the long term. The Communist states brought Marxism a bad name. But as the memories of this gradually fade, will the determinists have their day in the sun? Only time will tell. At this stage, it is worth noting that one of the prime advocates of the Marxist corrective approach, Alex

Callinicos, maintains that Stalin gave Communism a bad reputation by distorting the views of Marx and Lenin. But a more persuasive argument is that Lenin should be linked primarily with Stalin, not Marx; his 'weakest link' argument proved incorrect, yet he insisted on seeing the October Revolution as a socialist one and on forging ahead with Russian development under Communist rule.

Comparative theories of revolution

Another abstract way of explaining the collapse of Communist rule is to apply theories of revolution. There are many theories, and just two will be considered here. The first is the so-called theory of rising expectations. The basis of this theory can be traced back to the work of the 19th-century French historian and political analyst Alexis de Tocqueville, though he did not use this actual term. It has subsequently been adopted and adapted by many others, but is arguably most associated with Crane Brinton and James Davies. Basically, the theory states that oppression alone does not lead to revolution; if it did, there would be almost constant revolution in many parts of the world. Rather, it is when a leadership raises the hopes and expectations of the masses, which then run ahead of the capacity of that leadership to deliver – i.e. citizens become frustrated – that a revolution is most likely to occur. In many ways, this fits well with what happened in both the USSR and much of Eastern Europe, since Gorbachev raised expectations that then exceeded the Communist systems' capacity to deliver.

A second and more recent approach to revolution is that of American political scientist Charles Tilly. He argues that for a revolution to occur, there must be both a revolutionary situation and a revolutionary outcome. A revolutionary situation exists when there is a serious challenge from one or more quarters to the existing power-holders; the challengers seek to replace the existing rulers, and are supported by a significant proportion of the citizenry against state authorities that are either unwilling or unable to suppress the challengers. For Tilly, revolutionary situations do not necessarily develop into revolutionary outcomes. For this to occur, four conditions need to be met: members of the existing ruling group must defect to the challengers; the revolutionary challengers must have access to force; the military must either defect or at least be neutralized; and the revolutionary challengers must take control of the state apparatus. Many of these conditions pertained in much of the Communist world at the end of the 1980s. Unfortunately, Tilly found it difficult to apply his own theory to the anti-Communist revolutions of 1989–91. While he argued that countries such as Yugoslavia, Czechoslovakia, and the USSR had definitely undergone revolutionary change in the period 1989–91, he maintained that Poland and Bulgaria had only experienced 'marginal' revolutions, and he was uncertain about countries such as Hungary and Romania. This is a weakness of the approach.

One reason that many theorists of revolution have experienced difficulties in classifying the events in the Communist world between 1989 and 1991 is that most of the pre-existing theories considered violence a necessary component of a revolution. With notable exceptions – including Romania, former Yugoslavia, and parts of the USSR – the collapse of Communist power was relatively peaceful. This means that theories of revolution need to be revised, not that the events did not constitute revolutions. If a country was a *de facto* one-party state with a state-owned and centrally planned economy in the late 1980s, and by the early 1990s had several political parties competing for power and an increasingly privatized and marketized economy, it had undergone a revolutionary change.

Theories of modernization and dominoes

From the end of the 1980s, US political scientist and political economist Francis Fukuyama began to argue that the collapse of Communism had proven modernization theory correct. This theory first emerged in the late 1950s, when US political sociologist Seymour Martin Lipset published a seminal article in which he argued that there was a close correlation between democracy and the level of economic development. In an oft-cited quotation, Lipset maintained that 'The more well-to-do a nation, the greater the chances that it will sustain democracy'. Thus was born the contemporary version of modernization theory. Although there are almost as many variations on this theme as there are scholars who have written on it, the basic tenet is that at a certain level of economic development and per capita income, demands for democracy will be made, and that if those economic levels have been reached, democracy will endure. Although this argument has often been criticized, recent empirical analyses have largely supported it.

In the case of Communist states, modernization theory can be applied to argue that most had developed to such a point under Communism – in terms of industrialization, levels of education, and so on – that the time had come for the move to democracy. States that were not yet ready in terms of development were caught up in the general anti-Communist move 1989–91, in what can be described either as reverse domino theory or as a near reversal of Lenin's theory of imperialism.

The original version of domino theory was coined by US President Dwight Eisenhower in 1954, just after France had finally lost North Vietnam to the Communists; it argued that if one developing country in a region were to fall to Communism, its neighbours would follow one by one. It was often heard again in the 1970s as, within months of each other in 1975, South Vietnam, Cambodia, and Laos all fell to the Communists. The West was concerned that this could spread to Thailand, Malaysia, and other countries in the region – although it should be noted that the local Communists themselves had treated Vietnam, Laos, and Cambodia essentially as one since the 1930s, since all three were under French colonial control; this is reflected in the fact that a unified *Indochinese*

Communist Party had been founded in 1930. Clearly, the collapse of one neighbouring Communist state after another in 1989–91 can be expressed in the metaphor of falling dominoes; but they were falling *out* of Communism, not into it.

Lenin's theory maintained that revolution in Russia would trigger revolutions in its Western neighbours. In a sense, Gorbachev's *refolution* – a term coined by Oxford academic Timothy Garton Ash to refer to reform that mutates into revolution – triggered revolutions elsewhere in the Communist world; but they were *away* from socialism, not towards it.

A useful feature of the modernization approach is that it can help to explain why some post-Communist states have been largely successful in democratizing, while others have experienced difficulties, and have in some cases reverted to a version of dictatorship; by and large, it is the more prosperous post-Communist states that have enjoyed the greatest success in democratizing.

Legitimation crisis theory

The final theoretical explanation of the collapse of Communist power argues that Communists lost power because they had exhausted the means for legitimizing themselves and the Communist system. In short, they had lost faith in their own project and their right to rule. In the early 20th century, German sociologist Max Weber had argued that states legitimize themselves through one of three possible modes – traditional (e.g. the divine right of monarchs in Europe or the mandate of heaven in parts of East Asia), charismatic (especially following revolutions), and legal-rational. In the real world, he argued, legitimacy can be based on a mixture of these, but one of them is usually dominant. Weber saw the last of these three as the only appropriate way of legitimizing a modern state; it basically refers to a situation in which the rule of law (and arguably democracy) is paramount; nobody – not even the supreme leader – is above the law.

In theory, Communist states could not be legitimized on the basis of tradition, since that would have fundamentally contradicted their allegedly revolutionary nature. In practice, many incorporated nationalism into their ideologies, which often – and increasingly so over time – included references to the distant past; in a sense, this constituted a form of traditional legitimation. Some Communist states were able to legitimize the political system on the basis of the charisma of a revolutionary leader, such as Lenin in the USSR, Mao (in the early years) in China, and Ho in Vietnam. But over time, more bureaucratic leaders came to power, so that charisma was no longer a possible source of legitimacy. Moreover, since Communist states did not respect the concepts of either the rule of law or democracy as these are commonly understood, they could not legitimize themselves on the basis of legal rationality.

Legitimacy was not in fact a major priority to most Communist states in the early years of Communist rule; coercion dominated legitimacy as the primary source of political power. As the decades passed, however, the gradual moves away from coercion in most Communist states saw many of them taking greater notice of the need to legitimize themselves to their own people. One way in which they sought to do this was via a mode not envisioned by Weber, but identified by Australian political scientist T. H. Rigby. He argued that Communist states increasingly sought to legitimize themselves on the basis of goal-rational legitimation. According to this theory, Communists claimed the right to rule – legitimacy – on the grounds that they knew best how to take society to socialism and then communism (i.e. the ultimate goal) quickly and efficiently; after all, the Communists claimed to constitute society's 'vanguard'.

Unfortunately, many Communist leaderships were by the 1970s admitting that the path ahead might be rockier than they had earlier envisaged, and began to argue that their societies would have to be realistic in their aspirations. Thus was born the concept of 'realistic socialism'. But once they started to admit their limitations and fallibility, the Communists were undermining their own vanguard-based claim to the right to rule. Some moved towards nationalism as a way of seeking this right, and identified themselves increasingly as descendants of pre-Communist national heroes and/or leaders; this was very obvious in East Germany and Romania. In other cases, leaders sought to identify with earlier charismatic Communist leaders, and claimed that they were taking the country back to the path determined by those leaders; the best example is Gorbachev, who sometimes compared his own approach with Lenin's.

One other possible legitimation mode for the Communists was system performance, meaning that they would seek the right to rule by delivering what the people wanted. Unfortunately, the economic slowdowns of the 1970s and 1980s rendered this path problematic. Moreover, attempts to redress the balance between heavy and light industry – and thus between the defence needs of the state and the consumer needs of citizens – had been at best only partial in most Communist states. Many citizens looked to the West, and saw that lifestyles and access to goods were much better there. Since their own leaderships had essentially put the end goal of communism on the back burner by the 1970s with their talk of 'realistic socialism' and acknowledgement of shortages, economic performance could not serve the legitimizing function leaders had hoped it would.

In short, most Communist leaderships had by the 1980s essentially run out of legitimation possibilities. Since they had also by then largely moved away from the arbitrary coercion (terror) that had typified earlier stages of Communist rule, they had exhausted *all* their possibilities for claiming their right to rule and exercising power. They had reached a dead end.

The present and the future

During the 1990s, many observers declared Marxism and Communism dead. For them, Communism had been tried and had failed the test. But is this position justified? On one level, it can be noted that Communist parties or their successors have survived in countries such as Germany, Czechia, and Russia, and in many cases still perform reasonably well in elections. But we need to look elsewhere for more persuasive evidence that Communism is not dead. With the worst global economic crisis since October 1929 reaching a peak in late 2008, even anti-Communist triumphalist Francis Fukuyama (*Newsweek*, 8 October 2008) was asking whether the Chinese model might be increasingly attractive. Does *this* mean that Communism could be resurrected?

The first point to make in addressing this question is that it is now almost two decades since the collapse of most Communist states, in particular the USSR. The military threat to the West – the bogeyman – that Communism used to represent is dead. While threats of various kinds from Russia might have increased in the 2000s, they are from a particular country, not from a Communist system. And while the horrors perpetrated by Stalin, Mao, Pol Pot, and other Communist leaders must *never* be forgotten, it is time to move on from Cold War propaganda and acknowledge that Communism may have had some positive aspects, even if these were few in number. In short, it is time to look more coolly and objectively at the theory of communism and the practice of Communist power. In this context, a brief overview of recent Chinese developments is instructive.

From the late 1970s on, the Chinese Communists proved themselves to be both more pragmatic and more self-confident than their counterparts in the USSR and Eastern Europe. Supreme leader Deng Xiaoping and his successors all adopted policies that have enabled China to move away from the ideological fervour and imbalanced – though never *as* imbalanced as the Soviet – economy typical of earlier Chinese Communism. They pursued far more radical and successful economic reforms than those adopted in the 1960s and 1970s in the USSR and Eastern Europe. On one level these worked, in that Chinese growth has been consistently strong for more than two decades. In general, Chinese consumers have never had it so good. In this sense, China avoided the legitimation crisis experienced by their Western Communist neighbours by being able to base their own legitimacy on economic performance. In the process, however, they abandoned key aspects of Leninist Communism and, by the early 2000s, had a hybrid system that can best be described as post-Communist economically and socially, while remaining Communist politically.

Unlike their European Communist neighbours, the Chinese Communists never claimed that socialism, let alone communism, would be achieved relatively quickly. Whereas Stalin claimed that the USSR had achieved socialism by 1936, the Chinese Communists long ago stated that China would reach only the *first stage* of socialism by the 2050s. Nor have the Chinese been as overtly imperialistic as the Soviets were. All this helps to explain why, at the time of writing, they were still in power. But in as much as there is a fundamental contradiction between the Chinese increasingly capitalist economic system and its still Communist political system, there is what German social theorist Jürgen Habermas called a legitimation crisis. A system can tolerate such a fundamental contradiction as long as the economy is functioning well. In other words, many citizens in most types of system appear to be willing to tolerate limits on their political freedoms as long as their standards of living are increasing, their security is ensured, and they are reasonably free to travel. These preconditions have pertained in China for more than two decades. But if the Chinese economy were to experience a serious crisis, there are many precedents to suggest that the political system could fail.

It has already been noted that some East European leaderships sought to circumvent potential legitimation problems from the 1970s by appealing to nationalism, and the way the Communist authorities appealed to national pride before and during the 2008 Olympic Games represented a significant recent Chinese example of this. This may have been a sign that the leadership knew that legitimation based on economic performance could shortly face problems; since much of Chinese economic growth has been based on exports, recession in major trading partners means that even China could experience a marked decline in its impressive growth. Moreover, many Chinese – particularly in the countryside – have still not benefited much from the economic miracle anyway, and there is ample evidence of discontent in many rural and even some urban areas (e.g. where people have been forced to vacate their homes to make way for major new construction projects). Widespread corruption remains a source of social disquiet, as it had been during the 1989 crisis in China. In short, China had by the early 2000s moved a long way from the original tenets of Communism; but that would not necessarily save the Communists from a serious – and perhaps successful – challenge to their rule.

Other Communist states are also in a predicament. In 2008, the UN warned that high inflation and the impact of the global economic crisis could destabilize Vietnam which, like China, had been enjoying performance-based legitimacy for several years until then. Laos was also being affected by the global crisis, especially in its all-important tourism and garment-manufacturing sectors. Meanwhile, Cuba appeared uncertain of the way forward under its new leader, Raul Castro; and the North Korean system appeared to be as unwell and unstable as its leader, Kim Jong Il.

If one or more Asian Communist states and/or Cuba undergo revolutionary change, will *this* mean that the final nail has been knocked into the coffin of Communism? It is worth recalling that Marx had argued that socialist revolutions will occur only in highly developed states. He also maintained that such revolutions would have to occur in a number of states – there would have to be an *international* revolution – if they were not to be defeated by those they were seeking to replace. By October 2008, it was clear that the model of capitalism that had begun to spread in the late 1970s and had become dominant by the 1990s – variously known as neo-conservatism or Washington Consensus (in North America), neo-liberalism (in much of the rest of the world), and economic rationalism (in Oceania) – had failed dismally. But this does *not* mean that Communism will return. It is much more likely that a new hybrid that seeks to combine some of the better features of Communism (relative economic stability and security; greater economic and social equality) with some of those of democratic capitalism (relative freedom; scope for entrepreneurship and innovation) will emerge. Some have been seeking this for decades, usually by reference to the Third or Middle Way (i.e. neither Communism nor liberal democratic capitalism, but something that builds on the best features of both). During the 1990s, British Prime Minister Tony Blair and German Chancellor Gerhard Schroeder both showed considerable interest in the concept. Yet it received little popular attention. By the end of the first decade of the 21st century, however, there could be renewed interest in it. If there is, Marx might be proven correct in some important ways.

First, the interest and new approach will have emerged in part from the dialectical interaction of Communism and capitalism during the Cold War. Second, it will have also emerged as a reaction to the material problems caused by an excessively neo-liberal capitalist approach. In this sense, his dialectical materialist approach will have proved a useful way of interpreting developments. In addition, Marx's later writings, especially the incomplete *Capital*, provide many insights into what we now call globalization and how the 2007–8 global crisis arose. In as much as so much of the world, including many developing countries, looks to the developed states to solve the mess of the neo-liberal meltdown, Marx's focus on the developed world as the motor to a 'higher stage' might also prove correct.

However, just because Marx may have proved correct in *some* of his most general analysis and prognoses does not mean he had all the answers. No one thinker could have; to believe otherwise is to open the door to extremism and despotism. One of the greatest weaknesses in most Marxist analysis is its serious underestimation of the power of nationalism and other forms of identity politics. These are significant issues in the contemporary world, and future theorists of the Third or Middle Way will have to address them if any new hybrid model is to gain traction and credibility.

In considering the Middle Way, it is worth returning to the claim that the 21st century will be China's. China certainly has a hybrid system, and its own name for itself in Chinese – *Zhongguo* – translates literally as 'The Middle (or Central) Country'! Assuming it does not disintegrate, China will have to address identity politics too, and dramatically improve its stance on human rights, democracy, and the rule of law. If it does, its sheer size and rapidly growing influence mean that the rest of the world will have to take increasing notice of the way it operates. For a change, Fukuyama may have got it right in his October 2008 article; returning to the Wall-to-Wall metaphor at the start of this book, the Great Wall might act as a symbol of the future.

However, we need to consider the possibility that Chinese Communist power collapses, and that whatever succeeds it is, at least in the short term, unlikely to be a model others will seek to learn from or emulate. To conclude this brief analysis of Communism, it is finally time to acknowledge the elephant in the room – social democracy. In most countries in which voters were free to choose, social democracy proved to be more popular in the 20th century than Communism. The type of system Sweden had until the late 1980s – when even the Swedes began to move towards neo-liberalism – provides concrete evidence that it *is* possible to combine high levels of security, prosperity, the rule of law, freedom, and democracy. The hybrid has existed and could well return. For numerous reasons, it is both more desirable and more likely that it will experience a re-birth than that Communism will. But then that is how dialectics operate!

Further reading

The literatures on both communism as an idea and on Communist systems are vast. Moreover, it is assumed here that many readers will not have ready access to a university library, and hence to many specialized journals that contain invaluable articles. The suggestions here can only help take the reader a little further along the path to a better understanding of both communism and Communism; but almost all the sources cited here contain detailed bibliographies that can take the interested reader further still, and, for readers wanting to study a particular state in depth, many suggest readings on individual countries.

Chapter 1: The theory of communism

Two classic studies comparing communism as an ideal with Communism in practice are R. N. Carew Hunt, *The Theory and Practice of Communism* (Penguin, 1963) and A. Meyer, *Communism* (Random House, 1984). For two edited collections of some of the key texts of both Marxism and the debates within Marxist circles since Marx's death, see D. McLellan, *Karl Marx: Selected Writings*, 2nd edn. (Oxford University Press, 2000) and D. McLellan, *Marxism after Marx*, 4th edn. (Palgrave Macmillan, 2007) – while S. Avineri, *The Social and Political Thought of Karl Marx* (Cambridge University Press, 1968) provides a stimulating analysis of Marx's ideas. Standard works on Leninism include R. Tucker, *The Lenin Anthology* (Norton, 1975) and M. Liebman, *Leninism under Lenin* (Merlin, 1975), while N. Harding, *Leninism* (Palgrave Macmillan, 1996) adopts a somewhat unconventional approach. For Mao's theories, see S. Schram, *The Political Thought of Mao Tse-tung* (Penguin, 1969) or his abbreviated and updated later version, *The Thought of Mao Tse-tung* (Cambridge University Press, 1989). Stalin's ideas and impact are well covered in D. Hoffman (ed.), *Stalinism* (Blackwell, 2003), while readers interested in Eurocommunism should consult P. F. della Torre *et al.* (eds.), *Eurocommunism* (Penguin, 1979).

Chapter 2: A brief history of communism in power

For recent monumental overviews of Communism in power, see R. Service, *Comrades! A History of World Communism* (Macmillan, 2007) and A. Brown, *The Rise and Fall of Communism* (Bodley Head, 2009). On how Communists came to power in individual countries, see T. Hammond (ed.), *The Anatomy of Communist Takeovers* (Yale University Press, 1975). The standard text on the use of terror in Communist states is A. Dallin and G. Breslauer, *Political Terror in Communist Systems* (Stanford University Press, 1970). On the organizational principle of Communist parties, see M. Waller, *Democratic Centralism* (Manchester University Press, 1981), while a useful reference book on Communist parties is C. Hobday and R. East (eds.), *Communist and Marxist Parties of the World*, 2nd edn. (Longman, 1990). Finally, a comprehensive collection covering the history and politics of every Communist state is B. Szajkowski (ed.), *Marxist Governments: A World Survey*, 3 vols. (Macmillan, 1981).

Chapter 3: The political system of communism

Two introductory but detailed comparative texts are L. Holmes, *Politics in the Communist World* (Oxford University Press, 1986) and S. White, J. Gardner, and G. Schöpflin, *Communist Political Systems* (Macmillan, 1987). More advanced texts include L. Cohen and J. Shapiro (eds.), *Communist Systems in Comparative Perspective* (Anchor, 1974) and S. White and D. Nelson (eds.), *Communist Politics: A Reader* (Macmillan, 1986). Specifically on legislatures, see D. Nelson and S. White (eds.), *Communist Legislatures in Comparative Perspective* (Macmillan, 1982). Most Communist constitutions are included in W. Simons (ed.), *The Constitutions of the Communist World* (Sijthoff and Noordhoff, 1980), while those interested in reading the Communist party statutes of individual Communist countries should consult W. Simons and S. White (eds.), *The Party Statutes of the Communist World* (Martinus Nijhoff, 1984). Given their crucial importance, there is still too little on Communist Politburos; but for a detailed analysis of the Soviet one, see J. Löwenhardt, *The Soviet Politburo* (Canongate, 1982). Finally, comparative analyses of Communist leaderships include C. Beck *et al.*, *Comparative Communist Political Leadership* (McKay, 1973); R. B. Farrell (ed.), *Political Leadership in Eastern Europe and the Soviet Union* (Butterworths, 1970); and M. McCauley and S. Carter (eds.), *Leadership and Succession in the Soviet Union, Eastern Europe and China* (Macmillan, 1986).

Chapter 4: The economic system of communism

Specifically on the Soviet economy, see A. Nove, *An Economic History of the USSR, 1917–91* (Penguin, 1993) or P. Hanson, *The Rise and Fall of the Soviet Economy: An Economic History of the USSR 1945–1991* (Longman, 2003). A useful and accessible recent study of the Chinese economic system is B. Naughton, *The Chinese Economy: Transitions and Growth* (MIT Press, 2006). The somewhat different approach of the Yugoslav Communists is well covered in B. McFarlane, *Yugoslavia* (Pinter, 1988), especially Part 3. And for a feisty, more comparative analysis of Communist approaches to economics, see J. Kornai, *The Socialist System: The Political Economy of Communism* (Oxford University Press, 1992).

Chapter 5: Social policies and structures of communism

On class structures and the issue of equality in Communist systems, see D. Lane, *The End of Social Inequality?* (George Allen and Unwin, 1982). V. George and N. Manning, *Socialism, Social Welfare and the Soviet Union* (Routledge and Kegan Paul, 1980) is a useful study of Soviet social policies, while B. Deacon's *Social Policy and Socialism* (Pluto, 1982) provides a comparative analysis across Communist states. Valuable studies of Communists' policies on nationalism include W. Connor, *The National Question in Marxist-Leninist Theory and Strategy* (Princeton University Press, 1984) and P. Zwick, *National Communism* (Westview, 1983), while two studies that focus more on nationalism itself are P. Sugar (ed.), *Eastern European Nationalism in*

the Twentieth Century (American University Press, 1995) and
W. Kemp, *Nationalism and Communism in Eastern Europe and the
Soviet Union* (St Martin's, 1999). On gender politics and the situation
of women under Communism, see S. Wolchik and A. Meyer (eds.),
Women, State and Party in Eastern Europe (Duke University Press,
1985) or B. Jancar, *Women under Communism* (Johns Hopkins
University Press, 1978).

Chapter 6: Communism's international allegiances

For studies of Soviet foreign policy, see R. Edmonds, *Soviet Foreign
Policy* (Oxford University Press, 1983) or the slightly quirky (in
including an untranslated article in Russian) collection edited by
A. Dallin, *Soviet Foreign Policy 1917–1990* (Garland, 1992). On the
Warsaw Pact, see R. Remington, *The Warsaw Pact* (MIT Press, 1971),
and R. Clawson and L. Kaplan (eds.), *The Warsaw Pact* (Scholarly
Resources, 1982), while V. Mastny and M. Byrne (eds.), *Cardboard
Castle?* (Central European University Press, 2005) is an invaluable
source of key official documents. A worthwhile analysis of Comecon is
J. van Brabant, *Socialist Economic Integration* (Cambridge University
Press, 1980). Among the most useful studies of the Sino-Soviet rift are
W. Griffith, *The Sino-Soviet Rift* (MIT Press, 1964) and the much more
recent L. Lüthi, *The Sino-Soviet Split* (Princeton University Press,
2008). And a standard work on the tensions within the Soviet-
dominated world, but that also contains analysis of the Sino-Soviet
rift, is Z. Brzezinski, *The Soviet Bloc*, 2nd edn. (Harvard University
Press, 1967).

Chapter 7: The collapse of communism – and the future

For a country-by-country analysis of the collapse of Communist power,
see G. Stokes, *The Walls Came Tumbling Down* (Oxford University
Press, 1993). One of the best collections – in that it includes so many
different interpretations, including Fukuyama's – on the collapse of
Communist power is the special issue of *The National Interest*, No. 31,
1993, pp. 10–63 (for those who can access this journal). A classic study
of Gorbachev's role is A. Brown's *The Gorbachev Factor* (Oxford
University Press, 1996). A useful collection of essays on the role of
critical (Marxist) dissidents in the collapse of Communism is R. Taras

(ed.), *The Road to Disillusion* (M. E. Sharpe, 1992), while the best example of the Marxist corrective argument is A. Callinicos, *The Revenge of History* (Polity, 1991). The studies of revolution by C. Brinton and J. Davies referred to in the text are, respectively, *The Anatomy of Revolution*, 3rd edn. (Prentice Hall, 1965) and an article published in the journal *American Sociological Review* in 1962; the book by Tilly is *European Revolutions 1492–1992* (Blackwell, 1993). T. H. Rigby's argument about legitimation can be found in T. H. Rigby and F. Fehér (eds.), *Political Legitimation in Communist States* (Macmillan, 1982), while that concerning performance-based legitimation is elaborated in L. Holmes, *Post-Communism* (Duke University Press, 1997); Habermas' theory is in *Legitimation Crisis* (Heinemann, 1976). Finally, a thought-provoking analysis of the relevance of Marx since the collapse of Communist power is S. Sullivan's *Marx for a Post-Communist Era: On Poverty, Corruption and Banality* (Routledge, 2002).

Chronology

1818	Karl Marx born in Trier, Prussia (now Germany)
1848	Publication of the *Manifesto of the Communist Party*
1867	Publication of Vol. 1 of *Capital*
1870	Vladimir Lenin born in Simbirsk, Russia
1879	Josef Stalin born in Gori, Georgia
1883	Death of Marx
1893	Mao Zedong born in Hunan Province, China
1902	Publication of Lenin's *What is to be Done?*
1917	Publication of Lenin's *The State and Revolution*; Bolshevik (October) Revolution in Russia
1922	Union of Soviet Socialist Republics formally established
1924	Death of Lenin; Mongolia becomes second Communist state
1928	First five-year (economic) plan; Stalin consolidates power
early 1930s	Forced collectivization in USSR
1936	Stalin claims socialism has been achieved in USSR
1936-8	Height of the Stalin Terror
1939	Start of World War II; USSR signs non-aggression treaty with Nazi Germany
1941	USSR invaded by Germany
1945	End of World War II
late 1940s	Communism spreads throughout Eastern Europe and parts of Asia

1949	Mao and the Communists take power in China; establishment of Comecon
1953	Death of Stalin; mass unrest in East Germany
1955	Establishment of Warsaw Pact
1956	Khrushchev's Secret Speech; mass unrest in Poland and Hungary; Soviet invasion of Hungary
1957	Khrushchev consolidates power; USSR launches world's first space satellite, *Sputnik*
1958-60	Great Leap Forward in China
1961	Castro claims he is a Marxist-Leninist; East Germany erects Berlin Wall
1962	Cuban Missile Crisis
1964	Khrushchev ousted – new leadership in USSR under Brezhnev; US begins serious involvement in Vietnam War
1966-9	Most extreme phase of Cultural Revolution in China
1968	Prague Spring and invasion of Czechoslovakia
early 1970s	East – West détente
1973	US withdraws from Vietnam
1975	Reunification of Vietnam; Communists take power in Cambodia and Laos
1976	Death of Mao
1978	Deng consolidates power in China – start of major economic and social reform
1979	Soviet invasion of Afghanistan
1980	Death of Tito in Yugoslavia; Solidarity founded in Poland
1981	Martial law declared in Poland
1982	Death of Brezhnev
1985	Gorbachev becomes Soviet leader
1989	Completion of Soviet withdrawal from Afghanistan; start of collapse of Communism in Europe and elsewhere, symbolized by the fall of the Berlin Wall; Tiananmen Square crisis in China
1991	Dissolution of Comecon, Warsaw Pact, and USSR; Yugoslavia begins to break up
1997	Death of Deng

Index

C

Cambodia 66
  and China 114
  collapse of Communist power 51
  Communist accession to power 43, 130
  political parties, aspects of 60
  and terror 27, 68
  and Vietnam 50, 114–15, 116, 121
Callinicos, Alex 127–8
Capital 15–16, 137
capitalism, types of 69, 137
capitalists 4
Carter, Jimmy 40
Castro, Fidel 31–2, 64
Castro, Raul 136
Ceaușescu, Nicolae 101, 127
Charter 77 39–40
Chernenko, Konstantin 48
Chernyshevsky, Nikolai 7
Chiang Kai-shek 26
childbirth 101
childcare 101
China 42–3, 49, 81, 109, 111, 116, 123, 124
  Communist accession to power 26
  economy 74, 79, 80, 83–4, 118, 134–5
  gender aspects 99, 101
  mass unrest in 51
  military 64
  as model 134–6, 138
  police, security 63
  political parties, aspects of 53, 60
  social policies 86, 87, 88–9, 91, 118
  and terror 41–2
  and USSR 112–16
  see also Cultural Revolution; Great Leap Forward
China, Republic of – *see* Taiwan
Chinese, Han 95
Christian Democratic Union 62
church:
  Catholic 47, 96, 127
  Lutheran 127
Churchill, Winston 25
civil society 67–8
classes, social 4–5, 59–61, 93–5
cleavages, social 93–101
CMEA – *see* Council for Mutual Economic Assistance

collectivization 12, 20–2, 27, 71
Comecon – *see* Council for Mutual Economic Assistance
Cominform – *see* Communist Information Bureau
Comintern – *see* Communist International
communism:
  definition 5–6, 10
Communist Information Bureau 103–4, 110
Communist International 103
Communist Manifesto 4, 13
communist party 67, 95, 103, 132–3
  Afghanistan 60
  Albania 60
  Angola 60
  Benin 60
  Bulgaria 60
  Cambodia 53, 60
  central committee 55
  China 12–13, 53, 60
  Congo (Brazzaville) 60
  congress 55
  Cuba 53, 60
  Czechoslovakia 36, 60
  Ethiopia 60
  France 14, 104
  functions 56–8
  Germany (East) 53, 60
  Hungary 60
  Italy 14, 104
  Korea (North) 60
  Laos 60
  membership 58–60
  Mongolia 60
  Mozambique 60
  names 53–4
  Poland 53, 60
  politburo 55, 56
  role of 7–9, 56–8
  Romania 60
  ruling class, as 59–61
  secretariat 55–6, 58
  social composition 58–9
  Soviet Union 8, 18, 29–30, 49, 53, 54, 60
  Spain 14
  structure 54–6
  successors to 134
  Vietnam 60

Expand your collection of
VERY SHORT INTRODUCTIONS